Living in Words

R + R,
Best Wishes from your friends
and fans at [illegible].

Living in Words

Interviews from *The Bloomsbury Review* 1981–1988

Edited by Gregory McNamee

Breitenbush Books
Portland, Oregon

First edition. 2 3 4 5 6 7 8 9

Library of Congress Cataloging-in-Publication Data

Living in words: interviews from The Bloomsbury Review,
1981-1988 / edited by Gregory McNamee
ISBN 0-932576-62-1: Cloth ISBN 0-932576-63-X: Paper
1. Authors, English—20th Century—Interviews. 2. Authors, American—20th Century—Interviews. 3. English literature—20th Century—History and criticism. 4. American literature—20th Century—History and criticism. 5. Authorship.
I. McNamee, Gregory. II. Bloomsbury Review.
PR106.L58 1988 810'.9'0054—dc 19 88-12132

Breitenbush Books are published by James Anderson for Breitenbush Publications, Box 02137, Portland, Oregon 97202. Managing Editor, Paul Merchant.

Distributed by Taylor Publishing Company, Dallas, Texas.

Cover design by Susan Gustavson. Text design by Patrick Ames.
Manufactured in the USA.

The publisher and author thank the following artists, photographers, and publishers for permission to reprint the photographs used in this book, here listed in the order of appearance and by the writer's last name.

Boyle: © Phiz Mozesson. Courtesy of North Point Press.
Burroughs: © Marcia Resnick. Courtesy of the photographer.
Berry: © Thomas Victor. Courtesy of North Point Press.
Campbell: © Rhoda Pollack. Courtesy of the photographer.
Adams: © Michael Lichter. Courtesy of the photographer.
Moser: © Barry Moser. Courtesy of the artist.
Creeley: © Harry Munro. Courtesy of the photographer.
Mac Laverty: © Jerry Bauer. Courtesy of Grove Press, Inc.
Drabble: © Jerry Bauer. Courtesy of Alfred A. Knopf, Inc.
Mowat: © John de Visser. Courtesy of Farley Mowat.
Reid: Courtesy of North Point Press.
Nichols: © Richard Feldman. Courtesy of the photographer.
Carver: © Jerry Bauer. Courtesy of Random House, Inc.
Dorris and Erdrich: Courtesy of Michael Dorris and Louise Erdrich.

Table of Contents

Living in Words

Introduction

To speak of any human community is to name a body of people who share words and ideas, whose lives transform and are transformed by common purpose, who coevolve. To speak of a "literary community" in America today is therefore to risk calling out a phantasm, for nowhere, it seems, is there common direction and growth, shared responsibility and purpose, in the millions of words that are added each year to our literary culture.

For that reason, perhaps, many American writers are increasingly haunted by the sense that no one is listening, that words no longer matter, that to work with them is a failed enterprise; at least this is the sort of gloomy talk that one hears at writers' conferences and reads in the learned quarterlies. But consider the suppertime colloquia of Ralph Waldo Emerson, Henry David Thoreau, Nathaniel Hawthorne, and Louis Agassiz with the farmers and traders of New England; Mark Twain's lantern-lectures to anyone who cared to listen; William Carlos Williams's and Vachel Lindsay's public ministrations. And consider the hundreds of thousands of copies of books by "literary" writers — Ernest Hemingway, F. Scott Fitzgerald, William Faulkner — that graced the bookshelves of general readers in America in the years before the Second World War. Those writers understood that writing is never a solitary act, that a message must have not only a sender but also an understanding recipient if it is to have any meaning at all; as Guy Davenport has rightly remarked, "writing is the one social bond," uniting humans in ways that music, dance, and stock-car racing simply cannot. Those writers understood that one blames the archer, and not the target, for missing the mark.

It is not, as some fear, that no one is listening. It is that too many contemporary writers no longer serve an audience — as Barry

Lopez tells us, it is a writer's duty always to bow in respect to the reader — and no longer strive to forge with their work that social bond. Nor are those readers who sustain a love for words and free thought well served by the commercial publishing industry, by the popular media, by the academy, which offer literary trivialities in the place of substance. What the latest celebrity memoirist has to say about the state of the world is widely announced, the antics of undergraduate minimalists are accorded an attention appropriate to the national budget, and the overnight sensations of the university lament the presumed closing of the American mind. All the while, the work of scores of worthy writers (and the national budget, for that matter) is ignored, and the social bond grows ever weaker.

The Bloomsbury Review was founded in 1981 to provide a forum of a sort that did not then exist: a publication meant to define and serve a community of general readers and writers, and especially to call attention to books by writers who seemed rarely to attract widespread critical notice — books from university presses, independent commercial presses, and small literary presses, books published beyond the grey banks of the Hudson River. Those writers' intentions are perhaps best summarized by the poet and farmer Wendell Berry, who remarked to *The Bloomsbury Review* in 1983 that "a writer's responsibilities to the audience are to work to tell the truth and to work to keep the language fit to tell the truth."

What matters, given such a charge, is to keep one's hands stained in ink and smudged by newsprint, to keep one's eyes open, to speak out against the public lie. The fifteen men and women included in this book have been doing just that. For the better part of a decade, the magazine has worked to follow suit. Under the direction of Tom Auer, Marilyn Auer, and the late Steve Lester, *The Bloomsbury Review* has published conversations, in varying degrees of formality, with well-known and newly emerging writers. All of them, from Kay

Boyle, one of the first authors to be interviewed in the magazine, to Michael Dorris and Louise Erdrich, with whom we spoke in the winter of 1988, can fairly be said to share Berry's credo; if William S. Burroughs modestly likens his work to a woodsmith's craft — "Suppose you're making a chair ... you want to make the best chair you can" — and if Joseph Campbell happily attributes his many successes to the intervention of the Muses, they but report variations on Berry's theme, their own ways of arriving at the sense of responsibility and community that underlies all good writing.

It would not do for writers to give away all their secrets, not least because knowing them would destroy the innocent pleasure one takes from sitting down to read the elaborate fairy tale that is literature. These conversations report only the smallest part of a writer's work and concerns. For more, one needs to turn carefully to their writing itself, and, to this purpose, suggested readings accompany each of the following interviews. These handlists include only currently available books, in the editions one would most likely find today in any good general bookstore — which almost always means an independent bookstore.

For its part, *The Bloomsbury Review* continues to seek out new voices, new writers who daily advance, through their work, Wendell Berry's call of responsibility to truth and the language, writers who offer us the wide experience of their lives and imaginations to declare and nourish a true community of author and audience, the social bond that makes it possible, and even necessary, to live in words.

Gregory McNamee

• The Spirit of a Woman of Letters •

An Interview with Kay Boyle

Linda W. Ferguson

Born in St. Paul, Minnesota, in 1903, Kay Boyle first became known to American readers as an expatriate writer in Paris, one who lived and worked in the company of Ernest Hemingway, Archibald MacLeish, Gertrude Stein, Waverley Root, F. Scott Fitzgerald, Sylvia Beach, and especially Robert MacAlmon, with whom she wrote her memoir *Being Geniuses Together.* She later worked as a foreign correspondent for *The New Yorker.* Boyle has written some forty books.

Like many writers of her era, Boyle was drawn into the storm of McCarthyism in the late 1940s and early 1950s, and she was temporarily blacklisted. Boyle moved to San Francisco and took her place among the city's leading writers. When this interview took place in New York City in 1981, Boyle was preparing to move to Oregon and contemplating her work to come. She has since returned to San Francisco to live.

The Bloomsbury Review: You are thought of as a major writer of short stories in English. Yet you have published many novels and books of poems as well. Do you consider the short story to be your best form?

Kay Boyle: Definitely, definitely. I like to write poetry much better than I like to write prose. But I think that my short stories are very much better than my novels, and I've just recently discovered why. In most of my stories, I get away from myself. In my novels, there is always that American woman stalking around. She is disguised, but she is really me, and she is very boring. I think that the farther you get away from yourself — well, the way Beckett transposes his agony onto Estragon in *Waiting for Godot* or in *Krapp's Last Tape*. I manage to do that in my short stories. I did it only in one novel.

TBR: *Monday Night?*

KB: *Monday Night*.

TBR: Do you consider that your best novel?

KB: Yes. I did it, too — though not to the same extent — in *Generation without Farewell*. The protagonist was a German, but the American woman was in there, too, unfortunately. I said as much about this virtuous, boring woman in my introduction to the new edition of one of my early novels, *Plagued by the Nightingale,* which is coming out in England this spring. Here this ignorant young girl comes into her husband's French family and judges them from every point of view — for their Catholicism, for their conservatism, and so forth. And really, she was disrupting their lives. She, of course, is marvelous in every possible way, and all she can see is that she is an unappreciated, martyred creature. Anyway, I think that is why my short stories are more successful — that ability to get away from myself.

TBR: Your new collection, *Fifty Stories* under one cover, is very impressive.

KB: It is very expensive, too. You know, people don't go out and pay sixteen dollars for a book. And do you know what people in the trade say? In another three or four years, the way things are going, a novel will cost twenty-five to thirty dollars. No one is going to buy it. I think we have to admit that the capitalist system is on the skids. It's just not working.

TBR: Well, there is a lot of bureaucratic fat in the big publishing houses.

KB: The conglomerate syndrome is absolutely dreadful. Doubleday now owns the New York Mets, and Simon and Schuster is now owned by Dow Chemical. Obviously, they cannot justify the risk of printing the work of a young, unknown writer. It's out of the question.

TBR: Do you think this will mean a larger role for the small presses?

KB: My agent said yesterday that the small presses are in the same bind, really, because everything is going up — the cost of paper, the cost of labor, etc. They are going to have to charge much more than we are accustomed to paying for books.

TBR: Naturally, as an author, you see this most in books. What other changes do you see?

KB: I have just been in Miami for several weeks, visiting one of my daughters there. You cannot, absolutely cannot, cross the street in Greater Miami unless you are in a car. There is no way for a pedestrian. It's just like Los Angeles — the same horrible, sprawling network of freeways and expressways. It's terrifying and depressing.

TBR: You're leaving the San Francisco Bay Area for Oregon. It's hard to think of San Francisco without Kay Boyle, and vice versa.

KB: Yes, after seventeen years, I sold my wonderful old Victorian. My son, who was half-owner, took his share of the proceeds and bought a place in Cottage Grove just outside of Eugene, Oregon. He had moved up there to work, none of my other children were in the Bay Area, and I retired from teaching last December. There was no reason to stay. But I am going through trauma. You know, everyone said to me, "You're going to feel terrific shock." And I said, "Not at all, not at all. It's the logical thing to do, it's the right thing to do." Then as I was driving east from San Francisco, it suddenly struck me — I'll have no roots, I'm all mixed up. I don't know that I have any identity anymore.

TBR: But you are going to live in Oregon?

KB: Yes. My son's home is in a small town, and his land is right next to a national forest, so no one can build there. I think it's going to be wonderful.

TBR: And you are going to live in Ireland, too?

KB: I am going to Ireland for the summers, from the end of April or May till October every year, then back to Oregon. The winters in Ireland are a bit too rugged. It is not only damp, but all my friends had a difficult time heating their homes this last winter. They couldn't get any heating oil. It's a very tense situation there.

TBR: What part of Ireland are you going to?

KB: Dublin. I have many friends there. And I have friends in Cork, too. I love it, and I love the Irish people. I would like to be able to live there year-round, but it is not possible.

TBR: I understand Ireland has a wonderful tax set-up for writers and artists.

KB: There is some misunderstanding about that. It is only if you are a resident and buy property there, see? Someone who is over there only a few months a year could not possibly profit by that.

TBR: You're writing a book on Irish women, I hear.

KB: Yes, I have already started the book, and a couple of chapters have been published. In fact, one incident from the book was published in the *Atlantic Monthly* in June. And it was chosen as one of the best short stories of 1980. That made me feel as though I haven't lost my touch. You know, when you are seventy-eight, you are liable to lose a few things.

TBR: I can't imagine you losing anything. I just can't. You're a rock.

KB: A crumbling rock, let us say. You know, my editor at Doubleday just called and invited me to be one of the judges for the National Book Award this year. I said, "No, absolutely not." I'd have to read too many bad books. I have done it twice before, and I couldn't get back to my own writing because I felt the pressure of "I must read these books. I must." Now, were I younger, I probably would have accepted again this year. That's the other side, the more advantageous side of age.

TBR: Of the fifty stories, which is your favorite?

KB: Just off the top of my head, I would say "Defeat" because I was there at the fall of France. At the Academy of Arts and Letters last night, so many of my old friends said they liked "The White Horses of Vienna." And I suppose that one is all right, but I'm much closer to "Defeat."

TBR: "The White Horses of Vienna," of course, won the O. Henry Award....

KB: So did "Defeat."

TBR: In *Fifty Stories,* the stories are divided by different periods in your life, along geographical lines, such as "The Austrian Group," "The French Group," and so on. Do you consider yourself a cosmopolitan writer, a sort of citizen of the writing world, rather than, say, an American writer?

KB: No, I consider myself an American writer, very much so. I wish I could write an American novel one day. Maybe living in Oregon and getting closer to the soil, so to speak, I will do so. I want to very much.

TBR: My impression of you is that you have always been a city person.

KB: No, we hardly ever lived in cities — I can't stand cities. San Francisco is the city I have lived in longest in my life. I'm not a city person at all. We lived in the Alps, we climbed mountains, we crossed glaciers — so many of my stories reflect that. I was just in Paris on quick trips. I did have to work there for two years in order to support my little daughter, but I am not a city person at all.

TBR: I recently read a remark by Leslie Fiedler in *The Return of the Vanishing American,* in which he says that while other regions of the United States have produced definitive novels, the West has yet to produce one that is definitive, that integrates the Anglo consciousness with frontier or native consciousness. Do you agree?

KB: I think I do, right off the top of my head. Do you?

TBR: I am awfully fond of Willa Cather and Wright Morris.

KB: Oh, I'm not fond of Wright Morris's work at all. I have tried to enjoy it because we shared an office for many years, and he was always very nice to me, very helpful, but I have never cared for his work. Willa Cather is something else — I love her work. And as a child I used to sing her poetry. Oh, it's wonderful. Filled with the feeling of the Southwest.

TBR: Who are some of your favorite writers?

KB: Oh dear, that's a hard one. Flannery O'Connor, though of course she is dead. And I adore Eudora Welty's work. I don't like Joan Didion at all. I feel very angry about her work.

TBR: Why?

KB: I think it is cheap, trashy, egocentric. There is a wonderful essay on Joan Didion's work that appeared in *The Nation* in September of 1979. It is entitled "The Courage of Her Afflictions" because she writes so persistently about her various illnesses. For instance, the article quotes from one of her essays in which she discovers that the drapes she had ordered for her sitting room did not match her sofa. This horrendous discovery sends her to bed for two whole days with a migraine headache. Shall I go on?

TBR: Please do.

KB: Well, then there is an essay in one of her collections about the trial of Huey P. Newton, which I also covered — I did not see her there, incidentally, though of course I didn't know her then. In this essay, almost every fact is incorrect, wrong. Then, in a recent magazine article about the sixties, she brings in the strike at San Francisco State. For the incident between S.I. Hayakawa and me, which led to a well-publicized suit against Hayakawa, she relied on one hurriedly written, erroneous newspaper article, rather than on any accounts of the vast number of eyewitnesses. When I wrote her to correct this, she — or her secretary -- merely sent back a photostat of that one erroneous article with a scrawl across it to the effect that she was sticking by it. One depressing aspect of this is that many students last year were taking her as a role model, when there are so many good, really good, people around. I want women writers particularly to be awfully good, and it's depressing that she's so bad and so widely accepted.

TBR: Of all the writers I know, you are the most interested in younger, unestablished writers. Is there much happening among the young these days?

KB: There is a lot happening in the San Francisco Bay Area. I can't talk about New York because I haven't been there enough to know. But the Bay Area is quite active. I think some day the myth of Paris in the twenties and thirties will be reproduced again about the Bay Area. Paris was just as scattered, just as diverse as the Bay Area is now. Of course, no one has emerged from the Bay Area with the stature of a Joyce, but I think there is going to be the same myth about the Bay Area during the sixties and seventies — the eighties even.

TBR: There are various perquisites for writers — prizes, writer's associations, colonies such as Yaddo and MacDowell. Do you think such support creates more literary activity or better writing?

KB: I think support comes after you've accomplished a great deal of your work. For instance, at the Academy of Arts last night, most of the people there were my age or older. I think George Bernard Shaw once said of the Nobel Prize something to the effect that it was like a lifeline that is thrown to you when you are already sitting in the lifeboat. As for the writers' colonies, where you apply for a month's stay, there's no great honor or support involved in that. Most of the time, you have to pay. It's like going to a motel — a very nice, friendly motel, granted, where everyone else is working very hard.

TBR: What about writers' associations, such as PEN and the Authors' Guild?

KB: Now, I feel these are valuable for all writers to belong to. You learn a lot about the legal rights of authors versus publishers. For instance, currently the Authors' Guild and PEN are actively trying to persuade Doubleday to drop the suit against author Gwen Davis. You know, they are suing her for over $138,000.

TBR: I've heard something about you changing publishers over the matter.

KB: I'm not changing publishers. I just dropped Doubleday. I don't have a publisher. I returned the $1,000 advance they had paid me on *Irish Women*. There was nothing to be done about *Fifty Stories;* it was already in the works. Incidentally, there are three errors on the dust jacket of *Fifty Stories*. That's typical; Doubleday is known for its factual errors. First, I was not in Greenwich Village during the sixties. Second, I was not in Paris on the eve of the invasion. Any American in Paris at that time was in an internment camp. I was in the south of France, in the Alps. And I never taught at California State University, I taught at San Francisco State University. The name is completely wrong.

TBR: So all in all, you're finished with Doubleday?

KB: I wouldn't say all in all. I am still very friendly with Ken McCormick, my editor there. In fact, the editors gave me a dinner at the time I broke relations with Doubleday. I told them, "I don't think Doubleday should give me a dinner." They said, "You don't understand. We're the editors. We're not the people up there. And we're not in sympathy with Doubleday's stand."

TBR: What exactly happened in the Gwen Davis case?

KB: Well, she attended a nude encounter group, and later wrote a novel about it. One of the men involved thought he recognized himself and sued her and Doubleday, the publisher. Doubleday defended Davis's book all the way up to the New York Supreme Court. The suit came down against them. And then, they turned around and sued Gwen Davis. Naturally, the protests have been incredible. [Ed.: On November 18, 1980, Doubleday and Gwen Davis reached an out-of-court settlement. Both parties agreed that the terms of the settlement would not be disclosed.]

TBR: Are you the only author to your knowledge who has actually dropped Doubleday in protest?

KB: Actually dropped Doubleday? Yes, I tried to get other authors to follow suit, but they couldn't, just couldn't.

TBR: Don't you think that's because most authors are insecure about their next meal, even those who don't need to be?

KB: But it is a fact. Good writers, very good writers, simply are not making that much out of their books. None of them are. I think it is admirable that so many of them even protested.

TBR: Aren't you even a little insecure about being without a publisher?

KB: No, not at all. I'm absolutely free, which is very nice. Nobody is breathing down my neck.

TBR: Are you still active in political groups such as Amnesty International?

KB: Absolutely. That is the thing I am going to miss most about San Francisco. My group of Amnesty International has been functioning for six or seven years now and is supposed to be one of the most active groups in the United States. Group 80, a marvelous group of young people. Every year on my birthday, February 19, we have a benefit dinner to raise money. Last year, we raised nearly three thousand dollars, so many people came.

TBR: Are you going to come down to San Francisco for your birthday this year?

KB: I am indeed.

TBR: What do you think of Reagan as president?

KB: I think it's dreadful. And I don't know that it would have been any better had Jimmy Carter got in. And John Anderson had a terrible record. Everyone I know and respect, such as Dan Ellsberg, voted for Barry Commoner; he's a man of apparently great integrity. But the same thing is happening all over. I was in Paris in July, and over there it's the same thing. Nobody likes Giscard D'Estaing. They say, "There's nobody else around. Whoever we get in will be just as bad, if not worse." The world is in bad shape at the present.

TBR: Do you think war will come of it?

KB: I don't know. I think even Reagan is scared of war. I just hope to God he has good advisors around him. The most outrageous thing in his campaign was not warmongering, it was his speeches about what he did as governor of California. He did exactly the opposite of what he claimed he did. Taxes were never higher in California than when he was governor. As for the budget, he balanced it during the first several weeks he was in office, and then it just went out of sight.

TBR: This last election was obviously a mandate for the conservatives. The public seems strained by inflation, and fearful. Do you see this as a cyclical trend? I mean, do you think, say, ten years from now, the general public will again be as socially concerned and as vocal as it was in the sixties?

KB: Oh, I think long before ten years people will dare to speak up again and want to act together. But I think we are going to go through an awful four-year period. Possibly even McCarthyism will come back.

TBR: There is one final question I have to ask. Women writers with families often have difficulty making time to write. Yet you have been married three times and have raised, what, six children?

KB: Eight, actually. Two stepchildren and six of my own.

TBR: Eight. How did you do it?

KB: Frankly, I had help. During those early years, we lived in Europe, largely in rural areas in the south of France. And we could hire help very reasonably. I had help with the house and help with the children. It was really a matter of time and place.

TBR: In other words, you could not do that today in the United States? Raise eight children and still write?

KB: No, I don't think that would be possible.

A HANDLIST OF BOOKS BY KAY BOYLE

Monday Night (Appel Editions, 1977)
Fifty Stories (Penguin, 1981)
Three Short Novels (Penguin, 1982)
Being Geniuses Together (North Point, 1984)
Words That Must Somehow Be Said (North Point, 1985)
My Next Bride (Penguin, 1986)
Year Before Last (Penguin, 1986)
Life Being the Best & Other Stories (New Directions, 1988)

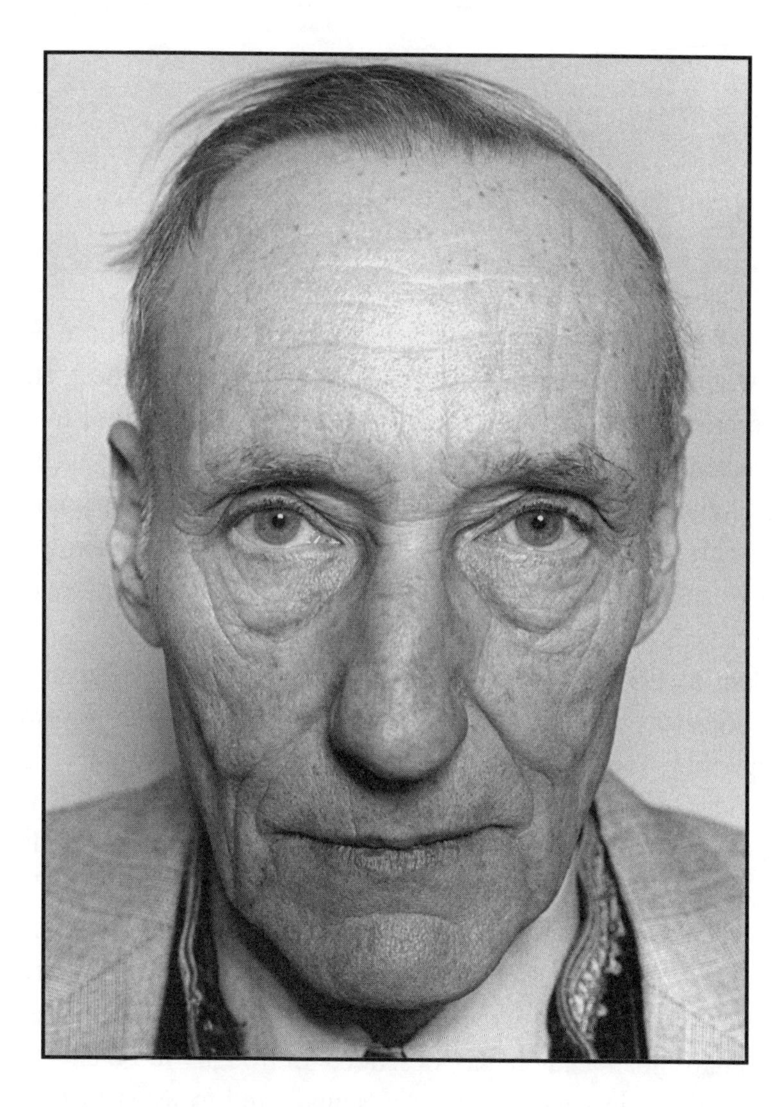

• The Writing of One Long Novel •

An Interview with William S. Burroughs

Tom Auer

William S. Burroughs occupies a peculiar place in American letters. His writings are taught in some schools and burned in others. He has been called, probably mistakenly, "the underground king of the Beat movement." Norman Mailer once said of him that Burroughs is "the only American novelist today who may conceivably be possessed by genius." Other critics have called his work "bogus-highbrow filth" and worse. Certainly his life and his writing have been informed by experiences that few can ever understand.

Born in 1914 in St. Louis, Missouri, and educated at Harvard and the University of Vienna, Burroughs has worked as an advertising copywriter, newspaper reporter, exterminator, factory hand, bartender, and private detective. He has been a professional writer since 1944. Burroughs has lived in London, Paris, Tangier, and Mexico City, where he first gained notoriety for killing his wife in a William Tell re-creation gone terribly awry. He was addicted to heroin for years, an experience reflected in much of his early writing. Burroughs is now writer-in-residence at the University of Kansas.

Perhaps Joan Didion has described Burroughs most effectively: "Burroughs is less a writer than a 'sound,' and to listen to the lyric may be to miss the beat."

This interview was conducted in February of 1981, in New York City.

The Bloomsbury Review: Could you tell us a little of your early years, and what the major influences were in your life that went on to affect your writing?

William S. Burroughs: Jean Genet once said that he started to write at birth. I think that is true of any writer. Long before he puts pen, pencil, or typewriter to paper, he is in effect a writer, filing his experiences away for future use. Well, my experience was something that hardly exists anymore — very comfortable, upper-middle class. We had servants. We had a yardman as well, a gardener, and a large comfortable house. Then we moved in the 1920s down into the suburbs where we had five acres. I was brought up there with hunting, fishing, guns. It was more or less a typical upbringing of the time. That whole world really doesn't exist anymore. Now I think you'd have to be a millionaire at least to have anyone cook your meals and put them on the table.

TBR: You really didn't start writing until you were about thirty. What made you take up writing?

WSB: Well, I had always wanted to be a writer and I tried several times before that and didn't succeed. And then in 1938 I wrote something in collaboration with Kells Elvins, a friend of mine, called *Twilight's Last Gleaming,* which has been one of the more successful pieces that I've used in my readings. A version of that appeared in *Nova Express.* I changed it to conform more closely to the original, which is a lot better than the published version. We sent it out and it was turned down everywhere. That was a period when I was very discouraged with the whole idea of writing, and then, when I was in Mexico around 1948 or '49, someone suggested that I write up my experiences about being an addict, and I started working on that and wrote a book called *Junky.* Well, when that was accepted, that gave me the impetus to go on. From there on I was more or less doing nothing else but writing.

TBR: Were you able to make a living at it?

WSB: No, no, my parents sent me an allowance — it wasn't a trust fund, as Kerouac said. They had a gift and art shop in Palm Beach. And they sent me two hundred dollars a month, which was quite adequate to live on outside America — in Tangier, places like that. But then in 1961 or thereabouts, I began really making a living. The first checks were coming in and they'd grow, made me think I was really something. From then on I was self-sufficient. I never had any money other than what I made from my writing.

TBR: What took you to Tangier? Was there something specific you were looking for?

WSB: No, it was just one of those places to go to, like Mexico City. I went there not knowing how long I wanted to stay, and I liked it and stayed there for five years.

TBR: You've traveled extensively in Central and South America, too.

WSB: I've traveled, yes. I lived in Mexico City a couple of years, and then I made a trip down through the Amazon, the Putamayo area of Colombia, and Ecuador and Peru. That was the extent of my travels.

TBR: Are you still in touch with Allen Ginsberg?

WSB: Certainly, certainly. Allen's a neighbor [in New York]. He lives about eight blocks from here, and I see him whenever he's in town. When I go to Boulder I always see him. He's always there in the summer. So I see quite a lot of him. I see quite a lot of Gregory Corso, too, when he's in town, although Gregory mostly lives in San Francisco. And I see Michael McClure from time to time.

TBR: How do you feel about the role you played as the "underground king of the Beat movement"?

WSB: I think that's a misnomer in many ways. When the movement really started in New York City with all the readings in the fifties and sixties, I wasn't here, I was in Europe. And my first visit to San Francisco wasn't until 1974.

TBR: How well did you know Jack Kerouac and Neal Cassady?

WSB: I was close to them at one time — in the late forties I met Neal and saw quite a lot of Jack when I would come to New York. And I saw them both in Mexico, Tangier, and Paris. In 1957, I saw Kerouac in Tangier — that was before *On the Road* was published, and then I didn't see him again until 1968 when I came over to cover the Democratic Convention in Chicago. I stopped in New York on my way back to see him. That was shortly before his death. I'll always have very good memories of Jack and Neal. I liked them both very much. They were good friends.

TBR: Were the roles Kerouac gave you in his novels based on fact?

WSB: Absolutely not. You see, his books were fiction. People assume that they're fact. He saddled me with a trust fund I haven't been able to get rid of. I never had a trust fund or a Russian countess. He was writing fiction. It may have been his conception of me, but it didn't have much to do with me.

TBR: In *Cities of the Red Night* you go back to a lot of the characters in your earlier novels. Why?

WSB: I am really writing one long novel in a sense, and so I tend to use the same characters. Most writers do the same — Graham Greene, for example, has one protagonist, really.

TBR: Do you write every day?

WSB: Yes, when I'm really working on something, I write every day. I start working at around ten in the morning and work through until six in the evening. I never eat lunch.

TBR: The jacket copy on *Cities* says you worked on it for ten years.

WSB: Nearer seven, really. I had the idea and I made some notes.... well, you could say I had worked on it for ten years, but the sketch for it was clear in my mind only for about seven.

TBR: Did you find it difficult at all to maintain your interest and stamina working on the book over that long a period?

WSB: Oh, yes, anyone does. There are moments when you reach an impasse and you may have to lay a book aside for a month, sometimes longer. There is no steady production over that length of time. And, of course, a great deal of the time I was editing. I would say that I was more than a year in editing.

TBR: How would you describe your place in contemporary American letters?

WSB: I wouldn't. In the first place, it's a known fact that writers have bad judgment. They often think that something is important that isn't. I would leave that judgment to someone else.

TBR: What kind of goals do you have as a writer?

WSB: Just writing, to do the best job I can. That's all.

TBR: To please yourself? Or do you have an audience in mind?

WSB: No, I don't have an audience in mind, and it isn't just to please myself. It's just doing the best job. Suppose you're making a chair. You want to make the best chair you can.

TBR: Is it easy for you now to make your living as a writer? Do you have other means of support?

WSB: The only other income I have is from giving readings and lectures. That forms a good half of my income. I suppose I wouldn't do it if I didn't have to, but I do.

TBR: Are you uncomfortable reading and lecturing?

WSB: Oh, no, I said I probably wouldn't do it if I didn't have to, like so many things. When I do it I thoroughly enjoy it, like cooking. I enjoy cooking when I do it, but if I were rich enough to have someone else do it, I probably would.

TBR: Are you still experimenting with your cut-up and fold-in techniques?

WSB: I do to some extent, if I'm stuck. I might cut up a page and get one sentence out of it, and then use it in a narrative.

TBR: Could you describe that process?

WSB: Brion Gysin said in 1959 that writing is fifty years behind, and he simply applied the montage method, which was old hat at that point. The painters sort of had their representational position knocked out from under them by photography. And there's no comparable invention that forced writers to change. So the montage method is closer to the facts of perception than representational painting is. Someone walks around the block of a city and when he comes back and puts what he's seen down on canvas, he's used jumbles of fragments. People cut in two by a car, that kind of thing. Gysin applied that same method to writing.

TBR: Do you think that's leaving too much to chance?

WSB: Life is a cut-up. As soon as you stick your head out the door or even look out the window, your consciousness is cut by random facts. This is simply a certain perception I feel should be represented in art.

TBR: At one time you kept a three-column journal. In one column you recorded your exact experiences, in another what you were thinking at the time, and in the third what you happened to be reading at the time. Do you still do this?

WSB: No, I don't really have time for that sort of experimentation. I'm working more or less with straight narrative.

TBR: Do you keep a journal of any sort?

WSB: No, I write dreams down, a dream journal, that's all.

TBR: It seems that in your work plot and characterization take a back seat to images. Is that by design?

WSB: I wouldn't say that was true. I think of myself primarily as a creative character. Like any novelist I think characterization is very important in my work, although there are mythological characters — well, there isn't character development.

TBR: Your writing has been compared to that of a number of literary figures — Eliot, Joyce, Swift. What writers have influenced you most directly?

WSB: Most directly, Denton Welsh, who nobody's ever heard of. He was an English writer who died quite young at thirty-one in 1948, and a lot of his books are out of print. He only wrote five. Aubrey Carsons, one of my characters, is Denton Welsh. I use his style quite frequently and consciously, and I find it very easy to write in his style. The other influences would be Graham Greene and Joseph Conrad.

TBR: Are there any particular books that moved you? I know you've written about *Lord Jim.*

WSB: *Lord Jim,* yes. But I've read probably everything of Conrad's. *Under Western Eyes* influenced me very much. There's a whole chapter in *Naked Lunch,* where Benway is interrogating Carl, that is quite consciously modeled on the interview between Mikulin and the protagonist — I forget, it was another Russian name.

TBR: Who are you reading now?

WSB: I read mostly popular books — airplane reading, I call it. I read everything that Frederick Forsyth writes. I just read the last Graham Greene, *The Human Factor.* I read a lot of assorted fiction, horror stories, that sort of thing. I've read Stephen King's *The Shining.*

TBR: Do you enjoy King's writing?

WSB: Yes, I think it's very good. In fact, I'm doing a sort of literary conversation with him at New York University.

TBR: Are you reading anyone else who's not a King or a Forsyth or a Greene, someone who more people ought to know about?

WSB: Well, yes, there are people like that. I would be quick to mention David Ohle, who teaches at the University of Texas. I think he's a fine writer. He's only been able to publish one novel, *Motorman*. I wrote the introduction for it.

TBR: A number of writers recently have commented that the state of publishing is none too good, that literature is taking a back seat to formula fiction. Do you agree?

WSB: Well, I think there are probably more books being sold now than there ever were. I couldn't agree with that. Bookstores are full of books and they're selling them.

TBR: Do you see films regularly?

WSB: Almost never. The last one I saw was *The Shining*. I have to be very sure it's something I want to see, and there are a couple I would like to see that I missed — *Satyricon,* and *Alien* for the special effects. But I rarely go.

TBR: Have you ever worked on a film?

WSB: No.

TBR: Any desire to?

WSB: Not particularly. I've made several attempts. There was a time when there was going to be a film based on *Junky,* but the financing fell through. It's axiomatic: you can never do anything unless you have enough money, as far as films go. And so that project collapsed. It never really went out in Hollywood. I think it was kicked around for ten years before someone finally picked it up, and so we may see some action yet on *Junky* — someone's just taken an option.

TBR: What do you think of the new conservative mood of the country?

WSB: Well, it's not really a mood of the country, it's a mood of certain people who have always had the same mood — mostly old Bible-belters who've been around since the country was settled.

TBR: Do you think that mood, that right-wing structure, is going to be around for a while?

WSB: I don't see it as a right-wing structure. People who talk about fascism and so forth have never seen fascism in operation. You're not about to be dragged out of your bed at three in the morning and taken out and shot, the way it happens in South America, particularly in Argentina. As far as the average citizen is concerned, America is one of the freest countries in the world.

TBR: Have we been at all spoiled by the freedoms we have?

WSB: Yes. All right. In the sixties people had very definite objectives. They wanted to end the war in Vietnam. They wanted decriminalization of marijuana. They wanted to end censorship. They got it. All three. That's nothing to complain about.

A HANDLIST OF BOOKS BY WILLIAM S. BURROUGHS

The Soft Machine (Grove Press, 1966)
The Ticket That Exploded (Grove Press, 1967)
The Naked Lunch (Grove Press, 1969)
The Job (Grove Press, 1974)
Junky (Penguin, 1977)
Blade Runner (Blue Wind, 1979)
The Exterminator (Penguin, 1979)
Port of Saints (Blue Wind, 1980)
The Last Words of Dutch Schultz (Seaver Books, 1981)
Cities of the Red Night (Holt, 1982)
The Place of Dead Roads (Holt, 1984)
Queer (Viking Penguin, 1985)
The Adding Machine (Seaver, 1986)
The Western Lands (Viking, 1987)

• The Art of Living Right •

An Interview with Wendell Berry

Gregory McNamee & James R. Hepworth

Wendell Berry is a writer and farmer who speaks to his readers always of responsibility, of aware participation in the arts of life, be they those of composing a poem, preparing a field for planting, raising a family, working for the social good, loving. He calls for wise and sympathetic use of the earth's resources, with good tools and appropriate technology; for the continuity of customs that have proven themselves indispensable to living well and humanely; for honesty and integrity of expression and action.

Above all, Wendell Berry urges us to take stock of ourselves in the world, to better our social and economic health, to pass on to our children a world worth living in and a language worth speaking.

Berry's career as a writer began in 1960, with the publication of his first novel, *Nathan Colter*. Berry has since written several novels and books of verse, as well as many essays on the economic and agricultural crises confronting us today. North Point Press of San Francisco is now reissuing his early work and is the publisher of Berry's current writing. For his distinction in poetry and prose, Berry has gained both a solid reputation as an artist and an ever-increasing audience. Edward Abbey has called him "the best essayist writing in America today."

This interview took place in February of 1983.

The Bloomsbury Review: You have written that "learning to write poetry helped me to see farming as a way of life, not merely as a 'scientific' technique." What do your farming and poetry have in common? Are you the same person writing poetry as you are, say, when plowing?

Wendell Berry: Farming and poetry are both, to a considerable extent, formal disciplines. In both one must be concerned for the way that things are joined together, in one's mind and art and in the world. Neither a farm nor a poem should be made at the world's expense; the world must not be looked upon as a supply of "raw material" for either. To my way of thinking, any made thing should be made in harmony with its sources, and all things so made will have much in common; they will tend to be analogues of each other.

I am not sure that I understand the second part of the question. If I am one person, then I must be the same person, whatever I do, and I have always proceeded on the assumption that I am one person. Sometimes because of work I need to be more than one person, and sometimes because of pleasure, I would like to be.

TBR: You've written novels, essays, poems. Have you come to prefer one form to another? Are there any subjects you would confine to one form, that would only lend themselves to a certain method of expression?

WB: It is a matter of using the proper tool for the job you have at hand. This sort of propriety is going to be defined somewhat by the available readers. I think that most readers now feel, and I do too, that the most direct, most economical way is the best way. And so one would not, for example, write a novel or a poem to discuss a problem of agricultural technology, because that would encumber the discussion with unnecessary details or effects. I don't prefer one literary tool to another any more than a carpenter would prefer a saw to a hammer. A saw is fine for sawing, but you can't drive a nail with it.

TBR: You've said that your poems represent your "least-flawed work." Would you still hold to that statement?

WB: I am becoming less interested in arriving at that kind of statement. It is obviously necessary to try to improve the accuracy of one's judgment of one's work, if only because of the likelihood of error in self-judgment. But the life of the mind and the imagination, I think, bears little resemblance to a contest. My various pieces of writing are not involved in a race for first place, but in something more like a neighborhood; they have been necessary and helpful to each other.

TBR: You seem to be more at home with short lyrics than with narratives.

WB: As has been pointed out often enough, the storytelling ability seems to have migrated from poetry to prose. I would like to see it restored to poetry and have written a few narrative poems, but there are difficult problems. How, for instance, do you tell a story in verse without either writing prosaic verse or making the verse itself too obtrusive? I wish I knew.

TBR: Which writers do you most admire? Have they influenced your own work?

WB: The companionship of other writers, living and dead, has always been precious to me. But there is no contest here either. To try to rank the writers to whom one is indebted is to risk both forgetfulness and error. The question about influences is another that I think I should not try to answer. It asks me to tell the whole history of my life and a good deal of the histories of the lives of my companions and teachers, and it expects me to be right about all of it.

TBR: With your essay "Poetry and Place" you rely more heavily on references to English literature — Shakespeare, Spenser, Milton,

Pope — and on techniques of formal criticism than you generally have in the past. Does this mark a new direction for you? Will you be working more with criticism and literary explication?

WB: I believe that I have always relied on literary ancestors. If that reliance had been absent from my life, I think that writing would have been absent from my life too. In "Poetry and Place," I was trying to understand what certain ones of those ancestors had to say about the proper human connection to the world. My subject was propriety, an old-fashioned concept that I think is renewed by our present ecological concerns; it has to do with the question of how one should act, given one's place both in the world and in the order of creatures. This question was a major enterprise of Western literature from Homer and the Bible until industrialism and romanticism began to mince intelligence into the modern specializations.

Now, for a poet such as Gary Snyder, the question of how to act in your place has become paramount again. Once it is acknowledged that there is a proper way to act, it becomes evident that there are acts that are not proper; it thus becomes possible again to think — to think intelligently — about human conduct. One is brought back to the realizations that so troubled the older poets: there are limits to human trustworthiness with power. We can see now that industrial use of fossil fuels should have brought us back to those realizations. Nuclear power has forced us back to them — if we have sense enough to be scared of our propensity to use reason to justify unreasonable behavior. In "Poetry and Place" I was writing as a man — as a father and grandfather — thoroughly frightened by certain human possibilities. And I was looking back to the old poets for instruction and encouragement.

TBR: How important is sense of place to you? Can you imagine having done the work you have without it, rootless, as so many of us are? What can city-bound people contribute to the marriage relationship you propose between individual and place?

WB: I have lived mainly in, and mainly know about, one little stretch of country in Henry County, Kentucky, and so I assume that my sense of that place has an inestimable importance to me. To imagine myself without knowledge of that place would be to imagine somebody else.

City people have places — have the earth underfoot — just like country people. In city and country, the most necessary job of work now is to recover the possibility of neighborliness between ourselves and the other people and other creatures who live where we do — both on the earth and in the local neighborhood. That work cannot be done by people who move often, just as it cannot be done by absentee owners, officials, and experts.

As long as there are economic connections between city and country — and there always will be — responsibilities are to be met at both ends. If farmers should produce food responsibly, then city people should eat responsibly. That means buying, so far as possible, fresh food that is locally grown and preparing it at home. And it means, when possible, raising a garden.

TBR: Guy Davenport, a neighbor of yours, has said that "writing is the one social bond and should be objective, useful, instructive." Do you agree? What are the responsibilities of a writer toward his or her audience?

WB: I don't know the context of the quotation, but I respect Guy Davenport and would not be in any hurry to disagree with him. Writing is certainly an indispensable social bond, and for most of us it is the one bond that ties us to our cultural sources. I don't know how a person in Henry County, Kentucky, could learn the stories of Agamemnon or King Lear except by reading. But the importance of writing as a social bond becomes evident in another way when we consider that our laws are all written; we are governed by the editing and amendment and interpretation of texts. And so in a democracy, if we are to have a democracy, the ability to read is paramount. When a society loses its ability to read, as ours appears to be doing, it loses its ability to re-read — that is, to re-examine and re-think — that is, to read intelligently — that is, to govern itself.

A writer's responsibilities to the audience are to work to tell the truth and to work to keep the language fit to tell the truth. This does not mean that I or any other writer can hope to be entirely truthful, but we must try to be. Anxiety about one's own honesty and the truthfulness of one's language is one of the necessary motives.

TBR: In a talk you gave last year in Colorado, you referred to yourself as a "forest Christian." Could you explain this term and relate it to your work?

WB: I used the phrase "forest Christian" to suggest what has been, for me, a necessary shift in perspective on the New Testament: from that of the church to that of the whole Creation. I don't want to sound too positive or knowing about this, because I hope to understand the problem better than I do, but I feel more and more strongly that when St. Paul said that "we are members one of another," he was using a far more inclusive "we" than Christian institutions have generally thought. For me, this is the meaning of ecology. Whether we know it or not, whether we want to be or not, we are members one of another: humans (ourselves and our enemies), earthworms, whales, snakes, squirrels, trees, topsoil, flowers, weeds, germs, hills, rivers, swifts, and stones — all of "us." The work of the imagination, I feel, is to understand this. I don't think it can be understood by any other faculty. And to live here very long or very well, humans now have to understand it. For us, it is not a question of whether or not we shall be members one of another, but of whether or not we shall know that we are and act accordingly.

TBR: In *The Gift of Good Land* you write that to "defend the small farm is to defend a large part, and the best part, of our cultural inheritance." What are the key points of that inheritance? How should we be transmitting them?

WB: As the rest of the paragraph makes clear, I was saying that values cannot be preserved by division, by specialization. When you have divided one kind of value from another kind, you have already begun the destruction of both. I don't think the small farm can be preserved only as an economic quantity or only as a political idea or only as a family home. The small farm is all those things and much more, too; to speak of it as if it were only one of them is to make nothing of it. Similarly, the idea of property becomes abstract, tentative, and vulnerable if we try to ground it only in economics or only in law.

In defending the small farm, I am defending the idea that great numbers of ordinary people should own property — not money or stock certificates or insurance policies, but real property, property that can give them direct practical support, the means to help themselves, and so make them to a proper extent independent, both in their domestic economies and in their minds. People who have a measure of economic independence can obviously afford to think and speak and vote more freely than people who do not. To me this modest idea of property is not just legal or political or economic, but is validated also by the long cultural memories and feelings that adhere to the idea of homeland — not a nation to be defended "patriotically," but a place personally loved in the particular terms of its hills and trees and streams, houses and households, where the knowledge and memories of grandparents can pass with clear local reference into the minds of grandchildren. The understanding that people need such places and should not be alienated from them for economic or any other reasons, goes back in our culture at least to the institution of the year of jubilee [Ed.: see Leviticus 25: 10-13], the fiftieth year, when all properties had to be returned to their original owners — an early and honorable example of an artificial restraint on the workings of an economy. Such ideas are best transmitted by parents to their children, older friends to younger friends. Schools and governments should not be trusted with them. If schools and governments become agents of an economy such as ours, then they become instruments of alienation. That is because alienated people — people without property and without neighbors — consume more industrial services and products than people who are not alienated. People who have no neighbors, for instance, must buy help. People who have neighbors have help. Claims for the benevolence of the industrial economy are disproved by the phenomenon of "unemployment." People become unemployed because of alienation from land and community. People who own even tiny parcels of land on which they can work for their own support, and people who own shops or have trades or skills directly useful to their own communities, are not going to be unemployed.

TBR: Former Secretary of Agriculture Earl Butz and the ideology he represented seem to have been favorite targets of yours for quite some time. Have agricultural affairs improved or worsened since Butz's time? What, if anything, should government be doing with regard to farming?

WB: The increase of farm bankruptcies indicates that the financial plight of farmers has worsened since Mr. Butz's time — and to a considerable extent because of his policy of "full production," which came inevitably to mean overproduction.

The government, I think, needs to recognize that any economy — "free" or not — is an artifact. It is "managed" for the good of somebody or other — for the general good, say, or for the good of a few. If there is a genuine wish to make it possible for a lot of people to own land, then government can do that. It can do it, first of all, by ceasing to favor the large landowners. The Department of Agriculture's new Payment in Kind program, for instance, will pay large farmers more per acre than small farmers. In a democracy, there can be no argument about that. It is simply wrong.

But it is wrong agriculturally too. Soil erosion is one of the most serious threats to this country, and one of its causes is depopulation of the farmland.

I don't know whether or not the government can be expected to see this. It can't see it, I think, until a lot of people begin to see it. In representative government, the government is likely to represent the blindness of the governed.

The government, for instance, thinks that national defense is making weapons, and the people go along and pay for it. But soil conservation is elementary national defense. So is people conservation. So is the conservation of culture and intelligence. So is the conservation of political liberty and of the economic independence of households and communities. If the nation is to be defended, it may need many fewer warheads and many more real shareholders, people who own homes, homesteads, small businesses, small farms.

TBR: Is it really possible, as you hope, for America to sustain and maintain a stable, hereditary, healthy farming population, given all the pressures exerted by our economic order and agribusiness? Where do we begin?

WB: We once had a chance to sustain and maintain such a farming population. Now we have a chance only to build one, starting with a farm population that is literally vanishing, for it is now less than three percent of the total population and still going down. That, of course, is a smaller chance. Though I see plenty of room for hope, I see little for optimism.

To begin the necessary change, we must first see what the real situation of agriculture now is: what it requires of land and people, and what it costs, not just in money, but in ecological, social, cultural, and economic results. Second, we must understand the meaning, the terms, the technology, the techniques, and the art of agricultural health. We must understand, for instance, that a good farmer's mind is not simple, but extremely complex and highly accomplished. Third, we must understand that all of us — city people just as much as country people — live from farming and therefore have agricultural responsibilities.

TBR: Your early work was brought out by a variety of small and commercial publishers, but of late you seem to have settled with North Point Press. Have you found a home there?

WB: Yes, I feel that I have found a home at North Point. The reason is that I am a small writer, in the sense that none of my books has been a best seller or made a lot of money, and North Point is a small business. What a small writer and a small business have in common is an interest in making money, if necessary, in small amounts. Their interest, in other words, is the same, and so they do not need to have an adversary relationship. A small writer and a big publisher, on the other hand, are adversaries necessarily, because the attention of big publishers is focused on big money.

A HANDLIST OF BOOKS BY WENDELL BERRY

The Rise (University Press of Kentucky, 1968)
The Long-Legged House (Harcourt Brace Jovanovich, 1969)
A Continuous Harmony (HBJ, 1972)
Clearing (HBJ, 1977)
The Unforeseen Wilderness (Kentucky, 1977)
The Unsettling of America (Sierra Club, 1977)
A Part (North Point, 1980)
The Gift of Good Land (North Point, 1981)
Recollected Essays, 1965-1980 (North Point, 1981)
A Place on Earth (North Point, 1982)
The Wheel (North Point, 1982)
Standing by Words (North Point, 1983)
Collected Poems, 1957-1982 (North Point, 1985)
The Wild Birds (North Point, 1986)
Home Economics (North Point, 1987)
Sabbaths (North Point, 1987)

• The Master of Mythology •

An Interview with Joseph Campbell

Joe Nigg & Derrick Jensen

"It would not be too much to say that myth is the secret opening through which the inexhaustible energies of the cosmos pour into human cultural manifestations."

With this revelation, announced on the opening page of *The Hero with a Thousand Faces,* his best-known book, Joseph Campbell began a lifelong study that would establish him as the world's foremost scholar of mythology. Like the myths and legends with which he worked, Campbell's writings sprang from human experience and its universal implications. Campbell followed the threads which run from the Bible to the Diamond Sutra, from the legends of ancient Europe to *Star Wars,* and he wove them together to form a single, grand epic such as other mythographers had only imagined before him. Born in 1904 in New York, Campbell was educated at Columbia University, where he placed as an Olympic track runner, and in Europe, where he encountered the transformative ideas of Oswald Spengler, Carl Jung, and Heinrich Zimmer. He taught for many years at Sarah Lawrence College, retiring in the 1970s to Hawaii. Campbell died on October 30, 1987.

The following interview took place in Denver, Colorado, in December of 1983.

The Bloomsbury Review: Your recent book *The Way of the Animal Powers* is the first volume of a projected four-part series, *Historical Atlas of World Mythology.* How does this work-in-progress differ from your earlier mythological survey, *The Masks of God*?

Joseph Campbell: This one has a totally different format. The marvelous thing here is that I don't think there has been another scholar anywhere who has had the good fortune to have a publisher who said, "How many pictures do you need?" And mythology is basically visual. So this opportunity to have hundreds and hundreds of pictures, the ones I choose, and besides them, those brand-new beautiful maps, opens a whole new prospect to exposition. I can say things here you can't say without visual accompaniment. And the form of this book is something I'm very much interested in continuing through what are going to be four volumes, to have the relevant text and pictures appear on the same page spread.

TBR: That is difficult to do.

JC: We're on our fourth book designer. That gives you some notion of how difficult it is. It's one thing to write a discourse on mythology, and it's another thing to present the images.

TBR: Most of your earlier books also include illustrations. What different dimensions do photographs add to your work?

JC: The only other book that I've done that was based on this principle was *The Mythic Image,* which is published by Princeton, and they turned its newest edition into a smaller format paperback where the pictures, now in black and white, don't do the communicating they were meant to do. I was allowed only thirty-two color prints there. Here I have hundreds. I mean, we're in another stratosphere. Really! And the problem is not simply to communicate the idea; I want to communicate the experience of these mythic forms. That's the main thing. Not only the discourse, but also the experience. Like a poem: reduce a poem to prose, and you don't have it. Mythology is poetry.

TBR: How did you come to write your first book, with Henry Morton Robinson, *A Skeleton Key to Finnegans Wake*?

JC: I wasn't interested in writing it. I was interested in reading it. My friend Robinson was the one who tricked me into writing a book, and he was a real pro. He knew how to write a piece. He came down to dinner with my wife and me one evening and said, "Joe, how's it going with *Finnegans Wake*?" That was about three weeks after the book had appeared. I had discovered Joyce in 1927 as a student in Paris. And so Robinson said, "Somebody's got to write a key to this thing, and it might as well be you and I." So I said, "Oh, no!" and he said, "Oh, yes." And so we arranged that I would be the authority on Joyce, although he knew Joyce very well, and that he would be the authority on how to write a book. And that was my first. Then Simon and Schuster, on Robinson's suggestion, invited me to do a book on mythology. That was *The Hero with a Thousand Faces,* which they turned down. And that's how I got started writing. I've been writing ever since.

TBR: *Hero* is your most popular book. Why do you think it did so well?

JC: Because it's a damn good book, and it opens things that people knew but didn't know they knew — that this whole world breaks through to the realm of what we call the Muses, those spirits that are the inspirations of the imagination and also the impulses to life. And this ridiculous positivism and prosaic approach to life that's characteristic of post-nineteenth century thinking just leaves people in a desert, what we call the Waste Land. In the 1960s, with LSD, people were finding that these powers symbolized in the myths or represented in the myths are actual in themselves. Well, since then the book has sold hundreds of thousands of copies.

TBR: Many of the mythological themes and patterns you identify in *Hero* appear in the *Star Wars* films. Would you tell us about your work with George Lucas?

JC: The *Star Wars* thing is really a special story. It's quite lovely. I hadn't seen a movie for thirty years. I mean, this is something I stopped doing when the talkies came. As a kid I had my heroes; my ambition was to be a synthesis of Douglas Fairbanks and Leonardo da Vinci. Then I went to Europe as a student, and when I came back the movies had become talkies, and presently they were color-film talkies. I expected them pretty soon to be walking in the room with you. But the fun of it was gone for me, where life was projected on a plane of silence and mind, you know. A Charlie Chaplin movie, you don't have anything like that now. It gave you a pitch into another dimension. And then, furthermore, I was deep into my scholarship. And then George Lucas came out to Hawaii to let me know that he was interested in my work and educational television and so forth. Then he invited my wife and me to his place in California, and we saw *Star Wars* in the morning, *The Empire Strikes Back* in the afternoon, and *Return of the Jedi* in the evening. And the next day we saw that delicious thing, which everybody seemed to know, but I knew nothing about, *American Graffiti*. Isn't that great? All those kids getting themselves into deeper water than they knew they were in. Then he showed us his first film, *THX-1138*. I was really, really impressed. This is a major career. Those giant strides from one film to the next.

And what impressed me so much in the trilogy was that he just continued the theme that was Goethe's in *Faust*. Is man going to be manipulated by thinking machines, or is the machine going to be in the service of authentic human life? That's the theme of the trilogy. What Lucas called the "Dark Power" — the machine is dominant instead of subservient. I was thrilled, anyway, to learn that my books had given Lucas inspiration.

TBR: The monomyth of the hero focuses and unites many disparate things.

JC: Yes. And at the end of *Jedi* you have the father-son atonement, where the son saves the father. I'm very proud that my books could have initiated something like that. I was delighted!

TBR: Twentieth-century writers have difficulty anyway because they don't have very many systems or models to work with. You've written about many writers — Joyce, Yeats, Eliot, Mann — who used myths to unify their work; the structures help, and your books are in a way handbooks for writers. They suggest some kind of form in this chaotic century.

JC: They do, and they are, not only to writers but also to other artists. Just last evening I was at a party in New York given for my eightieth year — I'll be eighty in a couple of months. Well, I felt, I hated to have that party. I thought, "Goodbye, Joe! Adios, muchacho!" But it was lovely. And there was from Martha Graham a word or two saying how much I had helped her, and from Richard Adams, who wrote *Watership Down* and *Shardik,* saying how my books had made a writer of him. And we have heard the story of George Lucas. And then *2001* was based on my books, too. Definitely *Primitive Mythology,* chapter one. When I saw it, I thought, "Oh my God, that's right out of my book!" Kubrick said so after it was made. So, you see, it's one thing to get the old structure of the hero myth, but now they're pitching it out into the void where it's possible for the imagination to go. You're not bound to historical fact. That's the problem here. You get bound to history, you lose the spirit. That's the problem with the Bible, by the way. Everything gets to be historical instead of spiritually activated. But the other thing about George Lucas is that he identifies the contemporary problem: machine or humanity.

TBR: You have an essay in *Myths to Live By* about the moon shot. There you talk of technology as the medium by which the imagination travels to a different dimension and is freed. So technology can work either way for us.

JC: That's right. I'm all for it! To those people who are against the atom and all that, I say, "No, no! You've got to accept whatever power there is and handle it. Don't be afraid of it." Every time there's a breakthrough there are positive and negative aspects of power. And the one who isn't afraid of it is the one who's going to control the world.

TBR: The positive and negative aspects of power seem to be a theme of *Hero*.

JC: That's right, and that's what Lucas pulled out of it when he spoke of the Dark Power, the dark side of the Force.... I knew when I hit on this that I had found something that could activate artists. I'm just writing for artists and for my students.

TBR: Do you see yourself as an artist, as a scholar, or as both?

JC: I'm a scholar! And my problem is to communicate my scholarship to a public. And my public is my students and their like. Everyone has to address someone. I find that there are many who are ready to receive the news, but then comes the problem of how you communicate. There are two modes of communication, and I've worked hard, I wouldn't say as an artist but as a craftsman, on both. One is giving a lecture, and I can give a damned good lecture. The other is writing. I was interested in writing when I was in prep school, and I had an elegant teacher, and I worked at it. So I started to learn how to write long before I learned what to write. And I'm applying the techniques, the craft part.

TBR: Did you ever write fiction or poetry?

JC: I wrote four poems when I was a kid in prep school, and they're still good. I'm basically not a fiction writer, who has to be interested in the way a shadow falls on your jacket, the quality and feel of it and all that. I'm just too much up here to be visual that way and sensuous that way. And my fiction is lousy.

TBR: In *The Mythic Image* you thank the Muses, and in your new book you declare a Muse for it. Is the Muse the subconscious?

JC: The Muses are the personifications of the energies of that unconscious system that you touch when you sit down as a writer. You just have to find them. When I'm writing, it's in two ways: one is badly, and the other is well. When I write badly it's dictated from up here, and that's the stuff that goes into the scrap basket. There's often a period of trial, pushing around to see where I can get that trapdoor to open. And when I hit it, it's almost physical, the feeling of opening a door, holding it open, not giving a damn for the critics or what they'll think or say. Meanwhile, I've thought out what's going to be in this chapter. All that has to be planned first.

TBR: In his preface to *The Nigger of the 'Narcissus',* Joseph Conrad talks about the artist descending into "that lonely region of stress and strife," the only place one can write well.

JC: Exactly what I've said, too. It's an actual experience, nothing mysterious about it. If you've never hit that level, well, then I guess it's mysterious. But if you have, it's not. The next problem is how to get there and how to make it serve the program that has been determined for it. Coomaraswamy describes the meditation of an Indian artist. First he studies all the shastras, all the textbooks on what a god — say, Shiva — should look like, what weapons and symbols he's to have in his hand. Then he pronounces the Sikh syllable of Shiva and goes into meditation. And then Shiva shows himself with those weapons that the artist knows should be there. It's not what, it's how, that makes the thing sing.

TBR: So writing is a kind of meditation.

JC: It is for me. Meditation sounds complicated, but it's really just waiting. When it's really going, I know about two words ahead what's coming. I try not to publish anything that's from any other center.

TBR: Even though you're dealing with a mass of scholarly material, one never gets the notion that you're struggling to pull all this stuff together.

JC: In a book like *Animal Powers,* there are about five different kinds of writing. There's a lot of writing that has just to do with historical fact. And it's very difficult to pull it together and then try to make it sing. The rhythm of the prose is at the very center of the problem. I wouldn't know how to instruct anybody, but it's terribly important. And that's why when some goddamned proofreader turns something around, as proofreaders very freely do, the top of my head blows off. I've sweated it out to have it that way instead of the way that it's been corrected to. Often what has been done is to restore a style that I have eliminated. It may be more rational, clearer, but there's no music.

Well, there's that kind of thing, the historical business. You can't imagine the number of facts and places from which they come. Then there's the translation. I do a lot of translating — from German, French, Spanish, and sometimes other languages such as Sanskrit. And with dictionaries around I can translate from almost anything except Japanese and Chinese. To turn all that into my prose, that's another problem. Then there's the business of taking a myth, which has been recorded by some anthropologist in a trite, dead language, what I call "anthropological pidgin." You know, they make believe that primitive people speak that way. They don't. The primitive languages are very complex, and they carry many meanings in a single word. Anthropological pidgin doesn't do it. Well, to turn that back into life, there's another kind of writing you have to do in a book like this. You don't realize when you're reading along that you're going over water, now over dry land, now over swamps.

Then there's the criticism of my colleagues. I try to homogenize it so it goes all in nicely. I've worked hard on my prose. Most scholars don't.

TBR: Do you think of a title before writing a book?

JC: No. The title for *The Hero with a Thousand Faces* came out about two pages before the end of the first draft. Before that, I called it *How to Read a Myth* or something like that.

TBR: Which probably wouldn't have sold as many copies.

JC: I know, not at all. And it wouldn't have told the story either. I wanted very much to use it for the work I'm doing now, the *Historical Atlas of World Mythology.* Well, I had written what is now the first volume plus about two-thirds of what's going to be in the second volume. These were to have been one volume originally. We realized it was too heavy a book, so we cut it down to what it is now, starting with what was to have been the second half of the first volume, "the planting people." As soon as we cut it — now, this was about three weeks before the whole thing went to press — I saw four volumes, and their titles came out like that. I had thought of it before as "The Nonliterate People" and "The Literate People." When you split it in half, each of these splits into an organic unit: the first, huntering-gathering people; the second, planting people; the third, the high culture-mythological periods; and then, from 500 B.C. — the dateline of Confucius, the Buddha, Aeschylus, Pythagoras — where mythology moves into gnosis, the primal philosophy.

I'd been working on these books for eight years, frothing in my mind over a title. After a friend said, "What are the titles?" I said, right off the top of my head, *The Way of the Animal Powers, The Way of the Seeded Earth,* and so on. That's it. Now, isn't that marvelous? Those are good titles, and out they came. That's what I mean by the Muse. I didn't think of them.

TBR: That recalls a phrase about the Fates that you quote in *Hero:* "The Fates guide those who will; those who won't, they drag." Are the Fates inside or outside?

JC: They're right in here. There's a very interesting word in English, namely *weird,* as in the three Weird Sisters. This is the whole problem of personal destiny. In Islam, there's the word *kismet,* which is the destiny put on you by God. Kismet — that's why Muslim warriors are so courageous. Nothing can happen to them that's not their destiny. And so they go. If they're to die, they die.

But there's that European word, *werden* in German, "to become." And werden is at the root of "weird." You become what you are potentially to be. This is translated as Fate, but it's very different from kismet. It appears in *Beowulf,* the earliest English epic, when Beowulf, as an old warrior, is about to go up against the dragon, and he knows he isn't up to it. But that's what his destiny is to do. I mean, he's the chieftain, after all, and nobody else can go in on that dragon. There's a line that to me is one of the most telling in Anglo-Saxon literature: "Wyrd was very near." Beowulf is sitting, thinking, pulling himself together to go into battle. "Wyrd," the terminal moment of his werden, his becoming — beautiful line!

TBR: One reason a lot of people externalize the Fates is to take pressure off themselves.

JC: Well, you see, it's a dimension that is not of your person. It's transpersonal. You open up something that is deeper than your own personal notion of yourself. Even though it's you, it's beyond what you know of yourself. And so it's experience that's coming to you. When I open up like that, it comes to me from down here. But someone else might read it as coming in from the northwest.

TBR: In *Hero* you talk about going so deep on the hero journey that you open up to all the world. Finally it is not solipsistic. As you said with the moon shot, we go out to go in, or we go in to go out. Either way.

JC: That's the old tantric and hermetic stuff. What is above is below. What's below you is around you. It's a technique to trick your mind into relaxing, to receive what we call inspiration.

TBR: Can you explain archetypes?

JC: Oh, yes! It's biological. Our biology, our body, is an organization of organs, isn't it. And the energy movements come through those organs, don't they. It's the conflict of the impulses of the various organs that constitutes a conflict of the psyche. The imagination is grounded in those entities that come from the organs. And so, in my view, myth is biologically based.

TBR: You seem to be a very happy and a very lucky man to have been able to do what you wanted all your life.

JC: I decided a long time ago that I wouldn't do a goddamn thing I didn't want to. I came back from Europe as a student in 1929, about two weeks before the Wall Street crash. I had five years without a job. In Europe, where I spent two and a half years as a student, I had started to work on the medieval problem and the Arthurian romances. I went over there to study Old French and Provençal, and then I went to Germany to study Middle and Old High German. Then I started to study Sanskrit, and India came in. The whole world opened up! I came back to Columbia with no money and no job, and I said, "I don't want to go back into this little bottle that I started out in. Things have been buzzing out there!" So I just went up into the woods for five years and did all I wanted to do in the way of reading, pulling all this stuff together.

Those years, your early twenties, they're when your star is twinkling. If I were to have put myself under the ceiling of Roger Sherman Loomis, with whom I'd been studying, then I know where I would have been. I'd have gotten the job at Columbia that was waiting for me, and I know who got the job, and I know what kind of a guy he was. This is wonderful too: to have seen the fork in the road, to have seen the one you took, to have seen the guy who took the one you didn't take. He had a wonderful academic reputation, but you'll never hear of him again.

My word for young people now who ask me is, follow your bliss. It'll come. Nobody's ever been on that road before, and so, where you didn't know there were doors, there are not only doors but palaces.

A HANDLIST OF BOOKS BY JOSEPH CAMPBELL

The Hero with a Thousand Faces
(Princeton University Press, 1968)
The Flight of the Wild Gander (Regnery Gateway, 1972)
Myths to Live By (Bantam Books, 1973)
The Masks of God (Viking Penguin, 1970-1976)
Volume I: Primitive Mythology
Volume II: Oriental Mythology
Volume III: Occidental Mythology
Volume IV: Creative Mythology
with H.M. Robinson, *A Skeleton Key to Finnegans Wake*
(Viking Penguin, 1977)
The Mythic Image (Princeton University Press, 1981)
The Way of the Animal Powers (Van der Marck Editions, 1983)
The Inner Reaches of Outer Space (Van der Marck Editions, 1986)

• Ultimate Questions and Galactic Whimsies •

An Interview with Douglas Adams

Christopher Larsen

Douglas Adams is an amiable Englishman whose conversation seems to run a few minutes behind his thoughts. The tall, Cambridge-educated author speaks about the best beer and pubs in England with almost as much enthusiasm as he does about the upcoming film version of his first book, *The Hitchhiker's Guide to the Galaxy*. His second book, *The Restaurant at the End of the Universe,* introduced more readers to Adams's whimsical cosmology, and the third book, *Life, the Universe and Everything,* opened to impressive sales on both sides of the Atlantic. Like the trilogy's first two installments, *Life* follows Arthur Dent, the last Earthman alive, through the trials and tribulations of an absurd universe, featuring flights of fancy and hyperbole that have given Adams something of a cult following. In a characteristic bit of good-natured subversion, Adams recently added a fourth volume, *So Long, and Thanks for All the Fish,* to the trilogy.

Anyone who has seen "Doctor Who," a BBC science-fiction television serial for which Adams wrote for several years, can quickly identify the uniquely British sense of whimsy in the Hitchhiker trilogy. Adams's longtime association with Monty Python's Flying Circus, though highly overstated by the press, also seems to have had an influence on the farcical nature of his writing. Critics characterize his books as parodies or spoofs of science-fiction clichés, a generalization Adams is quick to rebut, saying that his inspiration comes less from the science fiction genre than from the Anglo-American humorist P.G. Wodehouse, of Jeeves and Bertie Wooster fame. In 1984, Adams spent less than a week in the United States touring to promote *Life* before leaving for Australia to research an article on coral reefs for the London *Times*. He gave up some of his time in Denver for an interview with *The Bloomsbury Review*.

The Bloomsbury Review: Let's jump right into it. What are your plans for the future?

Douglas Adams: Well, they keep on changing, according to who asks me when. If you had asked me a few weeks ago I would have said that the most immediate plan was to do a new book about *Hitchhiker*. Since then the idea of — the firm offer of — the film of *Hitchhiker* has come up. And I think that probably now that's going to be my next project. It means being back in the same ring again. For years people have been coming forward and saying, "What about the film?" with a greater or lesser degree of seriousness behind it. But there certainly were opportunities where I could have gone and done the film. I wasn't certain; it has gone into every other medium, and I couldn't really see why to do the film. I mean, there's always the obvious reason: you hope it's going to make some money. And I'm not going to be pompous and say that's not a good reason. It wasn't enough reason, if that was the only reason we were going to do it. I want a little bit more. So, during the course of this year, a number of things have occurred to me about it, and suddenly the time seemed right. I suddenly saw how it could be, what sort of film it should be, how it would look, what it would be like, and then I became very enthusiastic about it, because I haven't seen a film like it before. It was difficult for a while; I was thinking about whether even to do it as a film, how much it was going to look like *Star Wars*, or how much it was going to look like this, that or the other thing. Suddenly it began to be very clear to me, actually, how to translate it into film. So suddenly I'm very happy to go forward in that direction.

TBR: I understand that you have some ideas about a computer video game in conjunction with the film?

DA: Well, yes, only because a curious thing has happened, which is that I suppose my stance has been not exactly anti-technology, but anti–self-defeating technology. I get very annoyed or impatient or regard as being stupid some of the self-defeating technology with which we surround ourselves. And I've really been sort of making fun of computers in the last few years. Then recently I acquired a word processor and actually began to see what it was that they could do. Obviously, a word processor is a very limited form of computer, geared to a very specific function, but nevertheless I'm beginning to get some sort of glimpse into this world. I'm becoming absolutely fascinated. It's a wonderful writing tool. And I begin to think, I really ought to find out more about computers. I mean, it's all very well to sit on the sidelines making fun of them, but I ought to know a little bit more. I'm hoping, as soon as I stop traveling again, to get myself a home computer and actually sit and work on that.

Now I have been approached with the idea, "How about a Hitchhiker video game?" and so I've been turning my mind vaguely in that direction. I think there's room for having quite a lot of fun there.

TBR: What would its name be?

DA: Well, my current working title is "Battle Towels."

TBR: *Hitchhiker's Guide to the Galaxy* and the ensuing trilogy began as a BBC radio series, but it seems to have collected other media accoutrements as the books have come out. Has this affected the original story?

DA: Obviously each medium makes its own demands on the material, so I sit down and completely rewrite it and reconstruct it, rather than sell the same basic incidents.

TBR: Are all three books a result of radio script versions?

DA: No. Each book has been dealt with completely differently. The first book was based on the first four episodes of the radio show. The next book was based on, in this order, episodes 7, 8, 9, 10, 11, 12, 5, 6, but completely restructured, a lot of new material put in, a lot of old material cut out. The third book I decided to write as a book, so that's all new; it hasn't actually been in any other form whatsoever. So, on the one hand, I'm continuing to write *Hitchhiker,* or have been up to now, and each different point has actually been a new approach — I'm trying to find a new way of doing it.

TBR: In *Life, the Universe and Everything,* in which Arthur Dent gets lost in time again and continues getting swept up in cosmic mayhem, it seems he becomes more of a victim than before. He's even more hapless and helpless.

DA: Yes. Not to be too personal about this, but the third book certainly takes some of its flavor from the fact that I was actually going through a bad period at that time. There were various things that were happening that made me very unhappy. I was certainly not in a very positive frame of mind when I was writing that book. And I think the book probably reflects this to a certain extent.

TBR: Many reviewers of your books label them as spoofs or parodies of science fiction and its clichés and devices.

DA: No, they're not, and I think that that's a strange thing to say because I think that just to parody a style — a book which parodies a different book — I just think is boring, just as a film that parodies another film is boring. I don't know if the same is true here, but in England, for years, there've been television programs that parody other television programs, and I just get tired of seeing parodies of television programs on television. And books which parody other books — it's boring, I mean, I'm not sufficiently interested in science fiction to want to sit down and parody other science fiction. The whole point of the thing is using the conventions of science fiction to parody everything else. I think the idea that they're parodies of science fiction is given the lie anyway by the fact — if I can make this point without sounding arrogant — that they've sold many more copies than most science-fiction books ever do. My books appeal to a much wider audience than do most science-fiction books. I think that people who say they're just parodies of science fiction are missing the point by quite a long way.

TBR: The covers of the *Hitchhiker* books consistently feature a maniacal, sneering face. Is it your view that we're largely victims of a mean and crazy universe?

DA: Well, I suppose that's something that does come across from the books, certainly. I have to talk partly about what comes across in the books, because very often I know more about my attitudes towards things as a result of seeing what I've written, rather than saying, "my attitude is such," and then writing it out. Sometimes it's as much news to me as it is to anybody else. So, I say, "Ah, that's what I think." Certainly, I think I try to put humanity in a larger context than we sometimes see ourselves in. We tend to think of ourselves as being largely in control of the universe we perceive. But then we only tend to perceive the universe that we actually think ourselves actually being in control of, and it's a rather larger affair than that. I think that's the point I've discovered I'm trying to make.

TBR: And within the larger context, you include the jabs at bureaucrats....

DA: Oh, yes, a lot of that. I mean, it's simply because one of the things that gets me writing — and I find writing very difficult, I find it very difficult to get down to, and when I do manage to get down to it I find it very difficult to do — one thing which usually gets me going is just being irritated by something. Now, that's not usually some colossal or major issue, but some piece of stupidity, some really irritating bit. Any time I've had dealings with the phone company, that tends to be a very fertile period. It's just dealing with one person or another, either on the phone or in a letter, who's just inept, and it just gets me so annoyed. So that sort of thing sort of gets me going.

TBR: *Hitchhiker's Guide* also includes a small swipe at literary pompousness when Arthur and Ford Prefect battle vile Vogon poetry with some hifalutin' critical jargon.

DA: Yes, "professional pretentiousness," such as what we were taught to toss off at a moment's notice at the university. Yes, that was really just having a go at a rarer target, not one, really, of great universality. On the other hand, people found it funny, so I must have touched something a little bit familiar there.

TBR: Most of your villains or bug-eyed monsters are not especially evil or malevolent.

DA: No, they're mostly parodies of attitudes.

TBR: They seem to be derived from fairly mundane sources.

DA: I suppose I have a go at things which annoy me, if they're little things, by casting them in a huge, gross, cosmic scale, sort of flitting them back. That's a lot of where it comes from. And usually I find if I try to make a point about something large-scale which I feel strongly about, it becomes very, very heavy-handed, and I always, always have to abandon it, but find that it is by tackling things that actually make me laugh at the same time that they make me angry, there seems to be a way in which you don't connect through to something larger. Certainly a lot of the things I've had a go at which are relatively small or local problems, maybe you put on a grotesque, say, or make fun in a particular way, and they do seem then to turn into something else, which I can't really define myself any better than anybody else can. But they do seem to achieve some kind of universality or whatever. One of the things that gets me very deeply upset is the whole question of the nuclear arms race, and the appalling sort of suicidal madness and illogic of it all.

Every time I've tried to get to grips with that and really lay out what I think about it in satirical terms, it never works. I just become leaden and heavy-handed, and I just can't quite get it. I'm determined to get it one day, because I think that the more people have a tougher go at that situation...you know, I think it's something we have to keep in the front of our minds the whole time in order to try to do anything about it. But I certainly haven't come up with any way that satisfied me of expressing the real fury and anger I feel about that. I really want to get to some point that will hit the nail very, very squarely on the head and make people go "ouch!"

TBR: The "Don't panic" phrase that first appears in *Hitchhiker's Guide* seems to have caught on with many readers, if only because it contrasts sharply with Arthur Dent's usual response to his predicaments.

DA: Well, I suppose in a way the words "Don't panic" are really to remind people of the fact that there is a very great deal to panic about. Now if you're walking down a street on an apparently normal day, and somebody says to you, "Don't panic," in that instant you may think, "Why, what's gone wrong?" I think that's one of the things behind it. Asking people not to panic is a way of reminding them that there's an awful lot we've got to be panicking about.

A HANDLIST OF BOOKS BY DOUGLAS ADAMS

The Hitchhiker's Guide to the Galaxy (Crown, 1980)
The Restaurant at the End of the Universe (Crown, 1982)
Life, the Universe and Everything (Pocket Books, 1985)
So Long, and Thanks for All the Fish (Crown, 1985)
The Original Hitchhiker's Radio Scripts (Crown, 1985)
Dirk Gently's Holistic Detective Agency (Simon and Schuster, 1987)

• Artist in Wonderland •

An Interview with Barry Moser

Rodger Rapp

Barry Moser is an artist who explores and exploits the realm of the printed word in a singular way. To him, a good book is much more than an artfully ordered series of words and ideas. What most of us think of as a good book can, if the Muses will, be transformed into a finely crafted and carefully orchestrated work of art, capable of surprising and pleasing the eye and the mind of the reader. It is Moser's province to exercise the magic that makes such surprise and pleasure possible.

Moser was educated at Auburn University and the University of Tennessee at Chattanooga. He then uprooted himself and went north, undertaking graduate study at the University of Massachusetts. There he taught himself the techniques of woodcut engraving, working for years to refine his ever-evolving craft. His distinctive, highly stylized illustrations, like the handset texts embracing them, have since earned him great critical acclaim, and he has brought new life to such classic works as Herman Melville's *Moby-Dick,* Dante Alighieri's *Divine Comedy,* Lewis Carroll's *Alice in Wonderland* and *Through the Looking-Glass,* Eudora Welty's *The Robber Bridegroom,* and Mary Shelley's *Frankenstein.* He now operates his own publishing house and printery, Pennyroyal Press of Northampton, Massachusetts.

Wood engraving, the illustrative technique that drew Moser into the allied art of fine printing, mirrors the prosaic "reality" of the senses in reverse. Engravers and letterpress typesetters, working with elements later reversed in the printing process (and thereby made readable for the uninitiated), share what Moser describes as a "formation of habits." The eye and the mind, faced with these inversions of sensory and mental perspective, necessarily become confused, a condition in which Moser thrives, knifing his way through to new visual universes. Consider Moser's eternally frozen wave on the opening page of *Moby-Dick,* his befuddled White Rabbit from *Alice in Wonderland.*

Painstakingly wrought, Moser's visions are both entertaining and instructive, demonstrating that mere words, whether we realize it or not, are not always enough.

The Bloomsbury Review: Tell us why and how you became an artist.

Barry Moser: I guess, like most artists, it was the one thing as a child I did pretty well. I didn't play football or baseball very well. I was a Southerner, and in the South a young man in the family is not encouraged in the arts. Usually it's toward the military, where I was. I went to military school for six years. It didn't stick, but it was very discouraging. I remember one instance where I was "apprehended" drawing naked women on the blank backsides of the illustrations in my Spanish textbook. I was hauled to the commandant's office and busted from the rank of sergeant to corporal for drawing naked women. This was the Bible Belt, and it was tough. I taught myself to draw relatively well, but never prizewinningly well.

TBR: How secretive did you have to be in those early years of training for art?

BM: Not too. It wasn't as though my family didn't encourage me. My mother and the rest were always fascinated by what I did, but it's always been, "Well, Charlie Thompson couldn't make a living at it. Why do you think you can?" So it began that way. Later on in college, I majored in industrial design first, because automobiles are very macho. That was okay. But at least it got me into the art department, and then from there into painting. I majored in painting the last two years.

TBR: What did you do then?

BM: I put myself through college the last two years by preaching. This was in Tennessee. I was a licensed minister of a Methodist church and preached the gospel in a very fundamentalist way. The Methodist church wasn't too particular, but more so than the Baptist church. But I'm talking about something I was doing twenty-five years ago. I could preach. I could assist at wedding ceremonies. I could bury people. But I couldn't administer the sacrament. I was going to go to the Vanderbilt Theology School, but I became disgusted, as it were, with the religious bigotry that I finally became aware of. The sects down there are so exclusive that Southern Baptists figure that Northern Baptists ain't gonna go to heaven. You not only had to be white, you also had to be whatever it was a particular group thought you had to be. The South is no place for an agnostic. Religion was a very big part of my life, and I think it still is, in more subtle ways.

TBR: How is an artist received as a preacher?

BM: That never really came up because I was simply majoring in art; my profession, of course, was preaching. During that time, 1960 to 1962, I was painting in the direct line of Cézanne and that school — very fragmented, painterly, highly chromatic stuff. Then I started teaching high school and prep school, which I did for seventeen years. I moved from the South, which was the first really significant event of my life. The South at that time was not what we would call a bastion of culture. So I left it for a variety of reasons, but all of them, I think, could be boiled down to the issue of bigotry. And not just racial bigotry, although that was certainly a part of it. I come from a long line of bigots; it was one of those things I began to sense very early on in life.

I remember an instance in a department store in Chattanooga called Miller Brothers. It was summertime, and I was hot and thirsty. I was ten. There was a line at the drinking fountain that said "White Only," but there was no line at the fountain that said "Colored." I couldn't figure out why my mother wouldn't let me get a drink out of that fountain. It didn't say "Colored Only," just "Colored." I couldn't sit at the back of the bus either. I was brought up with that kind of mentality. It was a difficult fight for me later on. There was an injustice, and something wasn't right in my mind, although I didn't hear the word Negro until I was eighteen. Coming out of that kind of milieu and moving to the North was a distinct shift.

There was sexual bigotry too. It would have been okay to be an artist if I were a woman because art is "effeminate." Down in the South a man was determined to be a man by how big a gun collection he had and how well he played football. That was the major concern: masculinity. To be a painter meant being "delicate" in one's craft and "sensitive" in one's demeanor.

TBR: When did you start making woodcuts?

BM: In 1958, when I was a student at Auburn, I saw some of Leonard Baskin's work. There was something magical about those things, something about the density and crispness of black. During my last year of college I was trying to learn how to make such woodcuts. I was in an art department where there were two people; one taught studio art and the other taught art history. The guy who taught studio art was and is a very good painter, but he didn't know anything about printmaking. He allowed me the latitude to try it on my own. After I graduated, I tried several rather embarrassing attempts at making wood engravings by reading what it was all about, although ultimately it didn't work. When I moved up to Massachusetts in 1967, I happened to land in the same area where Baskin lived. A friend, Louis Smith, knew Baskin and introduced me to him. I worked with Baskin for a while, but only in drawing. We didn't work with wood engraving, but it was through Baskin and through trying my own hand at doing the thing which I saw was so visually exciting to me — that crisp black and white thing — that I taught myself. I had also ended up in an area where I could buy the right materials. Finding the right wood and the right tools was the key. This happened in 1968 and '69.

TBR: What kind of prints were you making?

BM: Free prints, not book prints. I taught myself how to make etchings and wood engravings at about the same time. Etchings are a lot easier to do.

TBR: Did you do landscapes?

BM: Landscapes and figures. It's curious, though — we were talking earlier about where you begin. I was going through some old papers recently, and I discovered one of those "famous artist school" tests that you order from a matchbook, one that I had mailed off when I was eleven. You know, those real dinky things where you have half a barn drawn and you have to finish it. The curious thing to me was the last page where they ask you to draw anything you like, to find out what you enjoy doing. I recently took that page to my glazier and had him frame it. I hung it in the studio as a reminder. The comment is often made that I'm influenced in my subject matter by Baskin, but here is living proof from the age of eleven that it's not true, because here on this test is an airplane — something I don't draw anymore, although I still fly — a MIG 15, a Russian plane. There's a figure of a guy standing up and flexing his muscles; the figure is still an important part of my art. There's a tree, and all you have to do is look at *Through the Looking-Glass* to see how many trees I still do like that. And there's a gargoyle's head, which shows my early fascination with the bizarre, something that is still very much a fascination.

TBR: This is all one picture?

BM: It's all on one page, the drawing of an airplane, of the head, the figure drawing, the tree, all separate vignettes as an eleven-year-old would do. But these are all still themes that constantly come back in my work. They're the things I read a book to illustrate, the things I look forward to. Can I get botanical motifs in? How can I work botanical motifs into the *Inferno*? It's real tough when there ain't a lot of flowers down there. It's the same thing with figures and grotesques. That's why my books are so dark, I suppose.

The other thing I have hanging in my studio, I found when I moved from the South, is something I did when I was sixteen that one could loosely call calligraphy. It's a corny old saying that I thought was wonderful. I wrote it out in Old English and then took a match and burned the edges. It's really tacky, but I have it hanging up in the shop because there again it points out to me that even at the age of sixteen I was very interested in letters, in pages, in books as objects, not simply as things to read.

TBR: Is wood engraving well suited to your sense of the grotesque?

BM: Yes, I think it evokes that kind of imagery. Because of the nature of the medium, it produces a very dark image. If I wanted to do a pale image, why choose a woodcut to do it?

TBR: Do you think of the Alice books as grotesque?

BM: Lewis Carroll certainly did. He said himself that he was dissatisfied in his search for illustrators, because he couldn't find anyone with the "appropriate sense of the weird and grotesque." Those are his words.

TBR: The Tenniel illustrations seem only quaint.

BM: They certainly do. They're certainly not weird or grotesque. Carroll and Tenniel were constantly bickering. That's why "The Wasp in a Wig" was pulled out. Well, no one really knows why. [Ed.: Sir

John Tenniel grumbled that "a wasp in a wig is altogether beyond the appliances of art," and refused to illustrate Carroll's short episode. Weary of arguing the point, Carroll simply deleted the passage from *Alice*. The excised episode was discovered among Carroll's manuscripts and restored to his famous book in 1974; Moser was the first to illustrate it.]

TBR: What sort of editorial pressure does an illustrator face? What are the rules?

BM: Ultimately, I have none. In the case of *Moby-Dick,* Arion Press hired my hands. They didn't want my eyes, they didn't want my mind, all they wanted were my hands. The project, from the very start, was conceived of as providing a context, not interpreting the text, such as a stage designer or a set designer would do. It was a highly technical sort of job. For each illustration I first did a drawing, sometimes as many as twenty-five drawings for a single illustration. Those drawings would be photocopied and sent to the directors of four maritime and whaling museums and a marine architect. Each one of those five would examine each drawing. They would go through and circle things and write notes: "Wrong kind of block. The block was not a steel strap block in 1842 — it would be a rope strap block." They'd send all that information back, and I would have to make all the corrections. Occasionally someone would criticize the composition; a drawing would come back with a red mark across it and the comment, "Too dramatic!"

TBR: Was that frustrating?

BM: For me it was, because I have a sense of drama. I like dramatic images. I look at things from underneath and on top and inside out and upside down. Not being able to can be really frustrating. On projects such as the Alice books, since I'm the publisher, I have free reign. No one can tell me anything.

TBR: How did you get into book illustration and design?

BM: I've never had to go to a publisher with my portfolio and say, "Can I illustrate for you?" They've always come to me. My first book-related job was in 1969. When I went to teach school, instead of coaching football, which I did in the South, I worked with a theater, building sets. I came to despise it, because I was spending four or five months, several hours a day, building something that ended up being torn down. I like permanency — I build my books so they're going to last. At any rate, while I was working with the theater, I did posters for the plays. The University of Massachusetts Press then asked me to do a book jacket for them. Then they gave me another commission to do a book on wildflowers. It just started blooming, as it were. I've been in the business relatively few years — about fourteen now.

TBR: How did Pennyroyal Press come about?

BM: The *Moby-Dick* project got things rolling. I worked with one of the best printers in the country, and I illustrated the book — those are two factors. I can design books fairly well, that's three factors. The fourth is the money. As a matter of fact, the last line of the thirty-second chapter of *Moby-Dick,* "Cetology," one of my favorite lines, comes to mind: "Oh Time, Strength, Cash, Patience!" In five words, Melville got it all down, the whole difficulty of the artist's life. Enough time, enough strength to work, enough cash to put food on the table for your family, and patience, the great patience that it takes to wait until the idea comes. Anyway, we had all these things, but we didn't have the money. So my partner went to work finding ways to make enough money to produce *Alice*. We did it without any expectation of the kind of success it turned out to be. *Looking-Glass* was never planned, it just seemed to follow naturally, a logical extension. I did a softbound edition of "The Hunting of the Snark" as a giveaway. The deluxe edition of *Alice* carries it.

TBR: Is Pennyroyal a benign partnership?

BM: It's like a sexless marriage. We don't tell each other what to do. I don't presume to tell the partner who takes care of the business end anything. I don't presume to tell the partner in charge of production how to run the presses or what to print first. They don't presume to tell me anything. I have great artistic freedom. It's the one thing I have now that I generate work on my own. I now can say to someone who wants to commission an illustration that I expect a lot of artistic freedom, because there's no need to work. It's a wonderfully privileged place to be.

TBR: How do decide what you want to illustrate in a book?

BM: That's an interesting thing. I work in a very unexpected way. When I start with a book, first of all I read it and try to get a sense of how big I want the book to be. That's a basic step: do I want the book to be this big, or do I want the book to be *this* big? If I'm going to do a Bible, I want it to have some heft to it. (I didn't want *Alice* to be that tiny, delicate little book. I wanted it to be bigger, a folio. So I designed the book at the maximum size my printing press could handle, printing four pages at a time. The size was the first factor — I wanted to know how it would feel in my hand when it was finished and bound.) Then I select the type and get the specifications to the typesetter for the dummy.

TBR: *Alice* has a lot of white space.

BM: I had just been down to the library and seen a book printed in the sixteenth century. The printer had used red marginalia and set the type flush along the gutter and left the outsides ragged. I said to myself, "I want to do the next book like this." That's why I ended up with marginal notes. It wasn't that I felt I wanted to do an annotated *Alice*. That's been done. So I went about trying to find who in the country is a very fine Victorian scholar, who is witty and could add something that Martin Gardner didn't. That's what led me to James Kincaid at the University of Colorado.

Anyway, once the design is down and the type is set, I've got these long galley proofs. I reread the text several times and make my list of illustrations. Then I go through page by page pasting up the dummy, and I get up to the mad tea party. We have to see the Hatter and the Hare; those are important images, but having tea just won't do. That sort of anecdotal illustration just isn't of any interest at all to me. You'll notice that in all the illustrations, at no time do you see a group of figures together. And you seldom see a figure in a landscape. I like to pull out and concentrate on just one thing. So I see the Hatter and the Hare. How are they going to work? I don't know, except that I want them facing each other, so when I cut the type and paste it up, I leave myself three-quarters of a page for the Hatter and three-quarters for the Hare, and then go on pasting up the book without any finished illustrations.

Once the dummy is all put together it goes to the printer, and he starts handsetting the type and printing the book without any illustrations. So what I've done is to limit myself to this much space for the Hare's house, this much space for the Hatter, and this much space for his compatriot the Hare. Once that is all set up — what I call the typographic cradle — then I go back and start illustrating. I know that the Hatter is going to be in this space. What does he look like? That's where the whole process really begins. Whatever I come up with has to fit the space. There's no two ways about it.

TBR: Did Albrecht Dürer illustrate as a second step when he did his books?

BM: I would be surprised, in a way, because printing in the early sixteenth century was done with the block printed at the same time as the type, on wet paper, with a hand press that came straight down. If it was done in two goes, the paper would shrink from being damp and then drying and your registration would have been thrown all to hell. We go at two runs, but to maintain perfect registration the paper has to be dry. In the text we were working from for *Alice* — you can't say it's the definitive text because Carroll kept playing around with it all his life, changing things and then sometimes changing them back — we found a typographical error. We'd been applying contemporary standards of editing and come up with a unique text anyway, one that the Carroll people have not found distasteful, which surprised us. At any rate, somewhere was a period that needed to be a comma, one of those typos that are hard to find. We knew we were going into a trade edition, and it's easy to correct on film once you shoot from the Pennyroyal edition, but we said, "No! Ain't good enough." So we ran that sheet back through the press and stuck a comma over the period. You can't see it.

TBR: Did you make any other changes?

BM: If you look in *Alice* where the White Rabbit shrieks out Alice's name, her name is printed in red directly over his mouth. The reason for that comes from Carroll saying that the only color for Alice is red. So when the White Rabbit shrieks out her name, red is the color of that statement. I took that idea and used it in a different context, a different reference — we printed the word Alice in red right in the middle of a line. Our press can do that, whereas the way Dürer worked, you couldn't do that. I wouldn't be surprised if he ran into trouble in laying out the pages. You can't have a widow left over someplace; that's a no-no in fine print. You've got to back up a few lines, or go forward a few lines to pick up that space, especially if you're doing it like my *Frankenstein,* which we just finished. It has no paragraphs. Instead of paragraphing we just dropped in paragraph markers. Every page is a solid mass of type — no indentations. If you find one word left out, that means you have to go all the way to the end of the chapter to accommodate it. The problem of widows is, of course, eliminated. Often the only place to catch up to typographic problems efficiently is within an illustration. I can't be so precious as to think that another sixteen points at the bottom of an image is going to make or break it.

TBR: You're comfortable, then, with what's called "the supremacy of the text?"

BM: I don't take liberties with the text. I'm an illustrator. If Carroll says the Queen wears spectacles so big, one argues with neither Carroll nor the Queen. She has spectacles. What kind? That's up to me. Whether I'm looking up at her, down at her, whether I'm far away or close to her, that's all up to me, and that gives me the latitude I want or need. I don't have to portray Alice performing sexual acts, as Salvador Dali did. There's no mention of that sort of thing anywhere.

TBR: Do you find being an illustrator different from being a "fine" artist?

BM: I've never seen any image that I do for a book as being a work of art. That's not what I do. I don't particularly like to see my illustrations on walls, although I have a few on the walls around my place. Title pages and things like that I sometimes frame, but they're not conceived that way. They're part of a unit of images. The images collectively serve as one piece, plus its typographic cradle, plus its binding, plus its paper, and all that. The whole, the unity, is a work of art, not the individual images.

TBR: Once you've designed the cradle, how do you proceed? Do you start at the beginning of the book and work your way through it?

BM: Not necessarily. Sometimes it's a matter of size. I'll do the big illustrations first and the small ones last, or I'll do five big, then five small. The drawing stage requires more invention. That's when the stereo goes off and the kids walk a little more softly. When I'm engraving, the stereo is going and I can take a break at five and go to the kitchen and make supper. But when I'm drawing, it's different. When I get to doing something like that, I have to have quiet, because it's calling on all kinds of concentration. But when I'm engraving, it's craft. I can carry on a conversation or leave it for a while and then come back to it. When the hand is done thinking, time's gone by. I don't know if an hour has passed, or two hours, or six hours. That's the tedious part.

TBR: Do you get a buzz from it, though?

BM: Ain't no high like that. Not from the actual drawing, but when the drawing is done, and you step back. As Mozart said, inspiration is always *ex post facto*. You've done something, and later on you understand that you were inspired when you did it. I don't draw because I feel inspired. You don't wait around for inspiration to come. That's a lazy man's game.

TBR: Who are some of the *Alice* likenesses modeled after?

BM: Allen Mandelbaum, who did the three-volume verse translation of Dante that I illustrated, is the model for the Mad Hatter. Allen's sort of a crazy man anyway, probably one of the most stunning minds in America in terms of his poetry. I don't know if you consider John Ashbery's poetry excessive. It's not easy and it requires a lot from you. There's more narrative in Allen's work. He's a linguist — he speaks seventeen languages — and that level of language shows up. It's allegorical. I don't know what it means, it doesn't make any difference to me if I understand it or not, I love the words. But at any rate, Allen's kind of a madman, and he wears hats. I've never seen him without one.

TBR: Was the Hare done from life?

BM: Not exactly. The cat brought home, in the middle of the night, what I guess at one point had been a whole rabbit. She ate all of it except the head, which she left on the front steps. I said to myself, I'm not ready to do the Hare yet, but I'm going to be soon, so I took the head, put it in a plastic bag, and chucked it in the freezer, much to the dismay of my children. Every time they opened the freezer and saw this rabbit staring out, they looked at me and said, "You're so gross!"

TBR: While we're in this vein, can you tell us more about *Frankenstein?*

BM: I think *Frankenstein* is more valuable as the myth Mary Wollstonecraft Shelley invented than for its "literary significance." For me, it was not a very good read. When I started rereading it, I was thinking of it as a metaphor for our times. It seemed appropriate to me that the creation of a monster that cannot be controlled symbolized modern times, the nuclear age. But the more I got into it and the more I studied it, I began to realize that ain't what it's all about. You could certainly construe it that way, but then to take that as the jumping-off point, the pivotal basis for the illustrations, just doesn't make sense. Ultimately, *Frankenstein* is a woman's story of having babies and miscarriages — real tricky stuff.

When I do a book, one of the things I like to try to do is make a significant contribution to scholarship, something the private press in America doesn't do enough of. I'm not a scholar myself. I have no pretensions of being a scholar. I'm not even well-read. I've seldom read the books I'm going to illustrate until I know I'm going to do the job. I read *Dr Jekyll and Mr Hyde* two years ago because I want to illustrate it someday. I had read *Alice* before, but never *Moby-Dick* — in fact, I still haven't read all of it. I don't want to be accused of misinterpreting or misrepresenting the classics. But, at the same time, I'm trying to make more than just new pictures for old works.

A HANDLIST OF BOOKS ILLUSTRATED BY BARRY MOSER

Moby-Dick; or, the Whale by Herman Melville
(Arion/University of California Press, 1979)
The Aeneid by Vergil (California, 1981)
The Divine Comedy by Dante Alighieri (California, 1980-1984)
Alice's Adventures in Wonderland and *Through the Looking-Glass*
by Lewis Carroll (Pennyroyal/California, 1982)
Frankenstein; or, the Modern Prometheus
by Mary Shelley (Pennyroyal/California, 1984)
Fifty Years of American Poetry by The Academy of American
Poets, (ed. Abrams, 1984)
The Adventures of Huckleberry Finn by Mark Twain
(Pennyroyal/California, 1986)
The Wizard of Oz by Frank Baum (Pennyroyal/California, 1987)
The Robber Bridegroom by Eudora Welty
(Harcourt Brace Jovanovich, 1987)
The Ghost Horse of the Mounties by sean o'huigin,
(David Godine, 1988)

• Lifelong Commitments •

An Interview with Robert Creeley

Ray Gonzalez

American poetry, fifty years after the modernist experiments of Ezra Pound and T.S. Eliot, is now a substantial branch of world literature, although our poets today seem little honored or read in their own country. Pound, Eliot, William Carlos Williams, Robert Frost, and Charles Olson, among others, will be remembered as our classic poets of the first half of the twentieth century; the second will likely be governed by such writers as W.S. Merwin, Gary Snyder, and James Wright, and by such younger poets as Amy Clampitt and Gjertrud Schnackenberg. Robert Creeley lies somewhere between these two periods. He has written for more than forty years, beginning at Black Mountain College in the 1940s, and his work stands among the finest American poetry of the century, expressing as it does a lifelong commitment to the written and spoken word. "I look," he has said, "to words and nothing else for my own redemption either as a man or poet."

Ray Gonzalez interviewed Creeley in Boulder, Colorado, in the summer of 1984.

The Bloomsbury Review: You have not often taught creative writing, but recently you decided to offer a two-week writing workshop at the Naropa Institute.

Robert Creeley: I've had a hard time with writing programs for several reasons. Unlike the situation in music or the visual arts, in writing there is a lack of physically accessible materials. Poetry is so involved with a personal and emotional threshold in the saying of things that it is extraordinarily hard to dictate even general rules, because of the particular structures poetry makes use of. In the usual writing class, the models students will be using for their own measure of what they can do with a poem will often be as various as the number of people in the class. When I was a student in Delmore Schwartz's writing class years ago, he asked us to come to the next meeting with the name of the writer we deemed the most extraordinary and masterful in the English language. I think he presumed we would come back with a consensus like Shakespeare, but the fourteen of us came back with fourteen different heroes.

In the few writing classes I have taught, I worked with students whose imaginations were so far from my own and whose heroes were people who wouldn't be enemies of mine, but would be damn close in some cases, or else they were writers whom I knew very little about. I have learned a great deal from students about different writers. I have always felt that regular reading and fellow writers and peers give me a more active focus.

TBR: Why are writing programs so popular now?

RC: If I can say so, cynically, they are easy credit. The demands in a creative writing class will not be as difficult as those in a class on Milton.

TBR: Do you think the relationship between student and teacher in writing courses has changed much since the 1950s?

RC: I have always felt that a good way to start a student-teacher relationship is to approach unobtrusively a writer you admire and see if you can work with him without crowding his time. I used to solicit the opinion of William Carlos Williams shyly, but I never overtly asked him to read my poems, though I occasionally slipped one in at the end of a letter. If he didn't mention it, I wouldn't feel wiped out. I sent poems to Ezra Pound, too. He never really remarked on them, but I knew he had seen them, and I always thought it would be too egocentric for me to ask people like him to see my work.

The idea that a great writer is a good teacher is a myth. I learned a lot from Céline, but I don't think he would have been a very apt teacher. There are many writers I have learned from whom I would never anticipate meeting in the classroom. I have also found students studying with writers whose work they have never read, which is grotesque.

I think the best teachers of writing are not writers but readers. One of the great teachers of writing is Warren Tolliman at the University of British Columbia. He is not a writer, but he is a great reader and critic. He sponsored and developed a cadre of Canadian writers who've put western Canada on the so-called literary map — writers like George Bering, Robert Hoag, Fred Wah. Tolliman led them to good models. A teacher is interesting as a medium and not an end point, someone who shows you the way to something rather than say, "I am the way." A young writer friend of mine in Buffalo studied with J.M. Coetzee this past spring when Coetzee was there for a semester. My friend showed him a story he had written. Coetzee read it and remarked that it seemed a curious blend of "psychological realism" and some other particular mode of contemporary writing, but he never made it clear which parts of the story fit those modes. So my friend was reading his story over and over, trying to figure out the "psychological realism" in his writing. I could sense that Coetzee didn't want to talk about writing at all. The sense of writing I got came from elders like Pound who said, "You have to educate yourself." In talking to publisher friends over the years, I found that no one has ever said that writers trained in writing programs were better than those who were not.

TBR: What were your Black Mountain College days like?

RC: Things are far more political among today's students when it comes to competing with one another. In the 1940s, being a young poet meant facing social hostility and economic limitations. The company in classes back then seemed much more determined, because when you showed up in a writing class, you were already pretty desperate. We were really looking for one another's company. Alison Lurie, an old friend, and I were in various writing classes in college, along with William Gaddis and John Hawkes. That company was decisive. I remember meeting Kenneth Koch in class for the first time, and he invited me to his room, poured me some excellent sherry, sat me down in a very comfortable chair, brought out these tender, exquisite, typed poems on onionskin paper and withdrew while I read them. I remember that occasion very happily because it was so simple, and now I feel that these friends in college taught me more about writing than anyone else. They were the first to give me the active texts of Gertrude Stein, things like that.

TBR: Many little magazines have appeared in recent years and are very competitive in soliciting only the best poets or publishing only a certain group of poets until it becomes repetitive.

RC: The Associated Writing Programs are partly responsible for that. There was an article in a recent issue of *American Book Review* that took writing programs to task over the bland repetitiveness of many program writers who now get published. They may be seeking innocent approval, and I don't really think it's their fault, but all these programs are creating curiously generalized and bland writing that stays in a very simple area of understanding.

TBR: Have they hurt American literature?

RC: Well, one thing to look at is what kind of rapport this literature has with its community and what use it is to our society. There is a very solid, young poet here in Boulder named Martin Estrada who is writing about what it's like to be Puerto Rican. His poems involve very particular social information and continuity, and they will always be a measure of what someone writes about such things. The other question is whether literature today can survive as active information within the factors of the craft itself. If interest is lost in the social aspects of a literary work, but it is good writing, it will survive. Many of the great American writers of the nineteenth century — Thoreau, Hawthorne, Melville, Emerson — had remarkably small audiences in their time. There is a lovely quote from Thoreau in a letter to a friend, where he says, "I now have a library of nine hundred books, and I wrote seven hundred of them."

TBR: On the question of social significance, the last time Robert Bly was here, he said that it was time again for poets to speak out against what is happening in El Salvador and Nicaragua. He was one of the founders of Poets Against the Vietnam War in the 1960s.

RC: I agree that it is indeed time, but I also think it is always time to speak out, because it is hard to stay away from political concerns. I remember during the Vietnam War I had a dilemma, not so much of conscience but of how I could participate. I couldn't use the war directly as information in my writing. God knows why, but it just didn't work. I would try to make a poem deliberately involved with these issues, but in no way would it be as authentic as, say, one of Robert Duncan's or Denise Levertov's, who spoke out in the Sixties. My particular abilities were within a close focus of classic and domestic and communal ways people live together.

TBR: Some poets say it's hard for them to write a political poem, yet others say all poetry is political.

RC: I think all poetry is political in the sense that Williams meant when he said, "The government of words is our responsibility, since it is of all governments the archetype." Insofar as language is a human act, what one does with it is a political act. You can fake it, but the very order of a sentence is political. The rhetoric and syntax inherent in the language will tell you a great deal about the social and political situation of the people who speak it. A language that has no subject would express very different attitudes toward possessions, let's say.

But the language that demands that the subject come first demands a very particular political order. No matter what one writes about, the order implicit in the writing will be political.

TBR: Years ago, in your essay "A Sense of Measure," you said that the subject of a poem was not so important as the form or the deeper process that shaped the poem.

RC: Ultimately, the content will be dependent on how the saying of it affects the person who hears it. The power of the poet to affect the emotional state of his listeners is crucial. That's why Walt Whitman is one of the greatest, why he is still with us. It was that deeper force behind his motives for saying the things he did.

TBR: Many young poets get caught up in trying to find a personal identity or name for themselves instead of working on craft and shaping that first.

RC: That is the classic Anglo, middle-class burden of being programmed by American education and social behavior to excel. Pound once remarked that there was a time when news articles, like those in the *Times* of London, were not signed by the writers, and everybody accepted this, because those writers put the work ahead of making a name for themselves. Now the making of "stars" has a high priority among many writers. There is pressure to be different, distinct from all others around you. When I first started writing, in certain ways I was stuck with a singular way of writing that was awkward to me. My poetic style was recognizable, but it wasn't always a pleasure to be different from other poets. Sooner or later, one wants to write in the most accessible way one can, not simply to be heard by millions, but so that the words are so common that no one could not know they were there.

TBR: How do you feel about the fact that many poets have imitated your style over the years? Off and on you hear someone say, "This is like a Creeley poem."

RC: Ha! I remember talking to Robert Duncan once about imitators, and he said that, sadly, his imitators usually left him reading imitations of those parts of his poems that he liked least. It seemed easy to imitate the most successful aspects of his style, which he didn't like. My imitators don't seem to be as disastrous, but there seems to be too much constriction of words and style in many poets today.

TBR: Was Pound a real influence on you? Was he ever involved with *Black Mountain Review?*

RC: As I said before, he never really remarked on my poems, but he gave me a great deal of valuable advice when I was poetry editor of *Black Mountain Review.* He was always recommending new writers and was supportive of little magazines at the time. The famous example of his help in founding *Poetry* magazine at the turn of the century comes to mind. He said that a good literary magazine should be the center of an active circle of writers who could support one another, share their work with as wide an audience as possible, and not use the freedom to publish as a tool to serve the interests of an élite few. The incredible success of today's small-press publishers would have been impossible without Ezra Pound. He is the one to thank for the pioneering things he did to promote poetry, help new writers, and see to it that the work got out.

TBR: You used to be a publisher yourself, with Divers Press in the fifties. Have you considered starting a press again?

RC: No, those days are over. It's up to younger editors and publishers to do the work. It takes a great deal of work and commitment that I'm glad to give, but it's time for others to do the publishing. My inclination now is to concentrate on my own writing.

TBR: Your *Collected Poems* was recently published, gathering the work of several decades. There's a joke that when a poet comes out with a collected poems, people read them, then shelve them and forget the poet, because they equate the appearance of such a collection with the end of a poet's career. What was involved in putting your collection together? Does it give you a sense of relief, of being able to go on to other things?

RC: When it came time to put it together, I had various options. I could take things out of older, already published books, or I could try to rewrite poems that I didn't think quite made it before. The best principle I could think of was to collect things that were previously published in periodicals and my books. There are only ten poems that had not appeared before. It seemed ridiculous to tamper with them, because I was collecting and not re-creating. It would have been a curious falsification of history if I had tried to tidy up old work. Why not give whomever wants to read my work the complete record, including things that are interesting and those pieces that can be argued as being not so good? Once the book was done, I felt relieved that the poems were in a truly collected state. I was very pleased over the course of reading proofs and not finding old poems that I felt shouldn't be there. *Collected Poems* coincided with an emotional shift in my life as well — with the end of a long marriage, the move to the East, then remarriage. I've had two more books published since then, which made me feel that it wasn't the end, that I could move on to newer work.

TBR: Does a poet have to adjust his or her work to the audience?

RC: Not necessarily adjust to or accommodate the audience in some conscious respect — but it's hard not to be affected by the world. Of course, I can't change what I wrote thirty years ago to accommodate today's environment, which may itself change again in thirty years.

TBR: Along with *Collected Poems,* your *Collected Prose* was recently published. Does your prose work involve a different process for you from that of the poetry?

RC: Yes, and in some ways, the prose is harder to do. Since the late 1970s, I have tried to write prose again, and I have only one short story and a recurring irritation to write more. One good thing about the *Collected Prose* is that many of the books, like *The Island,* were out of print, and now, like the poems, they have a final, secure place. Also, I feel more threatened by the prose collection because, unlike the poetry, there hasn't been more to come since. I hope to write more prose, but the collection feels more conclusive than I would like.

TBR: There seems to be a resurgence of the short story as a form, and many poets have published some outstanding fiction.

RC: There's a very useful book called *Poet's Prose* that discusses, among other things, with great imagination, the relationship between prose and poets. It mentions Williams's prose, and John Ashbery's, and mine. There are young writers like David Antin, Ron Silliman, and Michael Davidson who recognize that prose, both syntactically and rhetorically, creates more open ground for experimentation than poetry. After you've been writing poems for a number of years, like it or not, poetry becomes an increment of stylistic habit that really needs to be broken. One of the most effective ways to move syntax around is with prose. All these writers create a kind of prose-poetry, but the writing really stands out on its own. It's a refreshing way to write, and there are kinds of feelings, for me at least, that are hard to express in poems. I can play with the language very comfortably in prose.

TBR: Have you read Raymond Carver's short stories?

RC: No, I haven't, and I guess I should. I've read Lydia Davis, Fanny Howe, and a number of the writers in the anthology *Contemporary American Fiction,* published by Sun and Moon Press. It is a fascinating collection. The experimenting these writers are doing is more interesting to me than Carver, who is more of a classicist.

TBR: Would you ever attempt another novel like *The Island?*

RC: Ha! I hope not like *The Island,* but yes, I would like to. I would probably do it like I did *Mabel, Presences,* and *A Day Book.* I would also like to get more involved with narrative and tell a more explicit story that would be directly accessible to the reader.

TBR: What are you working on now?

RC: Not much in the last six months, which have been chaotic for my family. My wife had a complicated pregnancy, but the baby was born healthy. It took a lot out of us. I also taught at Buffalo in the spring after having been away a year and a half, and that was demanding. We recently moved to Maine. It's been a hectic summer.

TBR: Has it been hard to make a living as a poet all these years?

RC: I've been very lucky. I've never had a great deal of money, but I've been able to make ends meet. Once I was complaining to Charles Olson about the precarious lives we led, and he looked me in the eye and said, "Bob, you are very lucky!"

TBR: Some people have the idea that famous poets can live off their fame and that it is a very romantic thing to run around the country getting paid large sums of money to give readings.

RC: It's a myth. A poet's income is meager. Poets will never make much money, even if it sounds like some get paid quite well. Book sales don't help, because a successful book of poems is lucky to sell two thousand copies nationwide. My *Collected Poems* did well, selling about four hundred copies a month for a while and forcing the University of California Press to delay putting it out in paperback, but my income from that was only about four thousand dollars. You can't live off that and support a family. My agent and taxes cut into my reading fees, so I have to teach to really make money. The great pleasure for a poet, frankly, is to publish what he or she prefers, to have the work kept in print, and to have enough public respect to be heard. That's about as good as it ever gets for poets.

TBR: Many young American poets seem to think that American poetry is all there is.

RC: I think that is because we are very isolated in this country. Many poets around the world are familiar with American poetry. Martin Estrada told me that, thanks to Ernesto Cardenal, handsome editions of American poetry, including the works of Whitman and Williams, are available to the Nicaraguan people. Poetry is everywhere for everybody. If a country like the United States acts like it is afraid of the emotions of its own people, then it will tend to push them aside and act confused when those emotions are recognized by others and made primary in their lives.

A HANDLIST OF BOOKS BY ROBERT CREELEY

For Love (Scribners, 1962)
Selected Poems (Scribners, 1976)
Hello (New Directions, 1978)
Was That a Real Poem and Other Essays (Four Seasons, 1979)
The Island (M. Boyars, 1980)
The Collected Poems of Robert Creeley
(University of California Press, 1982)
Echoes (Coffee House Press, 1982)
Mirrors (New Directions, 1983)
The Collected Prose of Robert Creeley (M. Boyars, 1984)
Calendar (Coffee House Press, 1984)
Memory Gardens (New Directions, 1986)

• Capturing the Whirlwind •

An Interview with Bernard Mac Laverty

Gregory McNamee

Although Bernard Mac Laverty now lives in Bowmore, a village on the Isle of Islay off the west coast of Scotland, his work has rarely left the setting of his birthplace: Belfast, the capital of Northern Ireland and scene of brutal sectarian conflict for four hundred years. The Troubles in Ireland have provided Mac Laverty with the theme of much of his published work, especially the novel for which he is best known, *Cal.*

Born in 1942, Mac Laverty, a Catholic, worked in a medical laboratory at Belfast University for ten years. He then took a degree in English literature, and he and his wife Madeline moved to Edinburgh, Scotland, where Mac Laverty taught high school for several years. There he began crafting the short stories later published as *A Time to Dance* and *Secrets.* Mac Laverty soon was recognized as an important artist in his adopted country, and in 1978 the Scottish Arts Council awarded him a major grant, used in part to finance the writing of a charming children's book, *A Man in Search of a Pet,* published in Belfast. Meanwhile, many of his early stories began to appear as television plays in England, Scotland, and Ireland. In 1979, Mac Laverty, Madeline, and their four children left Edinburgh for Bowmore, known chiefly for its round medieval church. (Local legend has it that the cornerless church affords the devil no hiding place.)

Mac Laverty has since been supporting himself through his writing. On Islay he wrote his first novel, *Lamb,* the moving story of Owen Kane, a young epileptic boy in a reform school who is kidnapped by his priest, Michael Lamb, the essence of the Good

Samaritan despite having lost his faith. The two flee Ireland for London, pursued by the police, and are soon driven back to Ireland, where Lamb, fearful that Owen's freedom will end, kills the boy. *Lamb* was soon followed by *Cal,* which established Mac Laverty's reputation internationally.

For ten weeks of the year, Mac Laverty is writer-in-residence at the University of Aberdeen, Scotland. The rest of the time he works away at a busy pace. With Mac Laverty's responses to this written interview, for example, came the following note: "Here are some brief replies to your questions. I'm sorry I didn't expand on them more but I have to be away tomorrow at the filming of *Lamb,* then to Aberdeen for a fortnight, then to Ireland for [the filming of the short story] 'The Daily Woman'."

Mac Laverty writes somberly of his unfortunate homeland, but while the sectarian violence and intolerance that has been at the heart of his work shows no signs of disappearing in the foreseeable future, he says, "I think that as a person I'm somebody who has hope.... I mean, there are so many beautiful things knockin' about."

The Bloomsbury Review: Most fiction writers, it seems, come into their craft circuitously through journalism, book reviewing, criticism, and other journeyman pursuits indirectly connected with purely creative writing. Instead, for ten years you were a laboratory technician in a medical clinic. What prompted you to abandon this profession and become a writer?

Bernard Mac Laverty: It is not just as simple as that. When I left secondary school I had passed examinations in English and Chemistry. Because my qualifications were not sufficient for me to go to university, I went job hunting. I was offered a job in the lab "in the meantime." The meantime lasted ten years. All that time I was reading and trying to write. In 1970 I gave up the job and enrolled as a full-time student of English; I got a degree and a teaching qualification after five years' study and went off to teach English in Scotland. I taught for five years and when I had enough money saved to float my family for a year I gave up teaching to write. I have now kept myself for four years as a writer. Bells don't ring every forty minutes in my house, and I prefer it this way.

TBR: How do your stories come into being? Did any particular events inspire you to write *Cal, Lamb,* and your other work?

BML: They come in different ways and at different speeds. One might begin with a paragraph, and if it's good enough I might want to carry on with it. Another I'll have the ending, a character, an incident. There is no set pattern. *Lamb* came about after I read a similar case in a newspaper. I was moved by it and asked myself the question, "How can somebody perform an act like that?" That is a good creative starting point. Some of the shorter pieces in *Secrets* I wrote in a day — and yet I worked on "Between Two Shores" for over two years.

TBR: Your characters seem somehow to be dislocated, rootless, divorced from their communities, whether in the Republic or in the Six Counties. Has the old community in Ireland given way to the "community of bastards" that Cal so greatly fears?

BML: Have you read William Trevor's story "The Ballroom of Romance"? The men in this story are a community of bastards. I have been to dancehalls and ceilidhs [Ed.: neighborly gatherings] where many of the characters I've written would fit in.

TBR: The idea of redemption — in *Lamb, Cal,* and many of your short stories — seems very strong in your work. Paul "Bono" Hewson, vocalist for the Irish group U2, remarks that "there is a battle, as I see it, between good and evil, and I think you've got to find your place in it. It may be on a factory floor, or it may be writing songs." Do you agree? Have you found your place in the battle with your work, and is that place a specifically religious one?

BML: I agree with Hewson's statement — if his view of what is good and evil corresponds with my own. He may have something different in mind. I tend to be fairly useless in an argument: I always sit with friends listening to their arguments and side with the last one who has spoken or shouted. Later it is possible that I could write these viewpoints down, incorporate them into fiction, and arrive at a more complex version of the truth.

Therefore I do have a place in the battle, however small, but I wouldn't say it was a specifically religious one.

TBR: *Cal* makes a splendid example of how a book can be faithfully made into a film without damaging the integrity of either. You mentioned that *Lamb* and "The Daily Woman" are now being adapted to film. Are you satisfied with the work of filmmakers in treating your books? How much involvement do you have in the filmmaking process?

BML: Yes, up till now I have been very pleased with the visual translation of everything I have done. The first thing was a television play of "My Dear Palestrina", and that was well done — it won an award for the best play on Radio Telefis Eireann [Ed.: the Irish national broadcasting service] that year. When I was first asked to write a screenplay of *Cal* I was warned off the idea by someone who knew about the business. "It will all end in tears," he said. But I didn't find it that way. The writer must build up a total trust with the director and vice versa. Pat O'Connor, the director of *Cal,* made the best film possible out of the material, and the script was wonderfully served by John Lynch as Cal — when I saw him auditioning for the part I knew immediately it was him — and Helen Mirren as Marcella. Some people have asked me if I wrote the book with film in mind. The only thing that struck me as cinematic was the vision of the disused cottage in the snow. This shows that I had a chocolate-box imagination, not a cinematic one. It was only when I began to write the screenplay that I realized there were many things which transferred fairly easily to the visual. The abattoir scene, for instance, where Shamie comes out to meet Cal and holding a bloody knife raises his hand to let the boy get cigarettes out of his pocket. This establishes so much — about their relationship, about employment/unemployment, about the violence that is to come, about the way that people's privacy is affected by Army searches, about the inarticulateness of the affection between father and son.

My involvement with the filmmaking process is directly proportional to how long it's been going — at the beginning, the script stage, it is total, but at the editing stage it is almost nil. This is sad but understandable. The director must be able to hone and cut his pictures the way a writer does his words. If the author was around at this time there might well be blood on the floor. A director who is sympathetic to the original story will come up with the right pictures.

TBR: *Cal,* book and film, is billed as a love story. Yet it seems to be in fact a statement that in Northern Ireland, love is now impossible, whether the romantic love Cal and Marcella seek or the simple love of life and community that would enable the shopgirl in *Cal,* under happier circumstances, to smile at hearing Cal say "Merry Christmas." Does this reflect your own belief, or am I reading too much into the story?

BML: I think a "love story" is a fair enough description, but it is a love story which grows out of the Troubles. The Northern Ireland situation is not just there as a colorful background. Without the violence and the guilt there would have been no story. Some critics were daft enough to think that it was too much of a coincidence that Cal falls in love with the woman he has helped widow. They missed the point. It is an attempt to make reparation which drives him to seek her out. No other woman would do. I think you are reading too much into the shopgirl incident. Dour people like this exist in any community and, paradoxically, I find them funny. Wit is one of the things that keeps people in Northern Ireland sane.

TBR: Cal McCluskey says many times to his IRA colleagues that he wants out of the cycle of terror and violence. Is your residence in Scotland a way out of that cycle, a willful exile? Do you foresee returning to Northern Ireland to live?

BML: My reasons for leaving Belfast were threefold. Most writers seem to go away and look back at the place and I wondered what that would do for me — at the time I had not published anything much. Also, in the early 1970s, Belfast was a tense and uncomfortable place to live. I graduated and was looking for a job and it seemed the wise thing to do to look for a job elsewhere. I was offered a teaching post in Edinburgh and accepted it. Yes, I could well go back some day, but I don't know when. As Madeline, my wife, says, "We'll not be buried among these ones."

TBR: Like your contemporaries in the United States, many Irish and English writers seem to depend on university appointments as a supplement to their often tenuous incomes. You are now writer-in-residence at the University of Aberdeen. Does this appointment stand in the way of your craft, distract your creative powers from the writing at hand? Are the universities, in your view, desirable places for writers to work?

BML: The good thing about my appointment in Aberdeen is that it only lasts ten weeks per year (and lasts only two years). So when I go there I abandon all thought of writing, except for the two lectures I have to give. Me giving lectures to academics! It's like being asked to play the viola in front of the string section of the Berlin Philharmonic. So I just go down market, play the comb and paper, play the fool.

TBR: The literary critic George Steiner once complained that James Joyce had exhausted the possibilities of Irish English and the

Irish experience, that all subsequent Irish writers merely labored in Joyce's shadow. Is it possible for a contemporary Irish writer to work apart from Joyce's influence?

BML: Who's James Joyce?

TBR: Well... which writers, living and dead, have influenced your work? Among your contemporaries, Irish, European, and American, whom do you admire, recommend, learn from?

BML: I suppose everybody I've enjoyed reading has influenced what I write. There were very few books in our house. They were kept in a glass-fronted case the way the good china was — and they were used about as often. When I did start to read it was the Russians who grabbed my imagination first — particularly Dostoyevsky. Later it was the quiet of Chekhov. My regard for the short story began with reading Michael McLaverty and I was very impressed with Hemingway when I realized what he was up to. That fellow James Joyce is also quite good.

I think that the best short stories have been written by the Russians, Americans, and Irish. Americans like Sherwood Anderson, Flannery O'Connor, Bernard Malamud, and Tillie Olsen are all wonderful writers.

TBR: What are your methods of composition?

BML: I like to write in longhand first, score out, draw arrows. Then I type it all up. Recently I have been having a go at a word processor, and once you forget that it is a word processor it is very good. The problem with it is that it produces too clean a draft. Everything comes out like a *Reader's Digest* circular. There is still something to be said for a messy page.

It is difficult to say how many drafts I go through. Each time you look at a page you want to change words. Time might be a better indicator: for instance, both novels were written in about three months, and then I worked on each of them for about a year.

TBR: What do you have in mind for the future? Can you foresee writing a book without an Irish setting?

BML: I am trying to build another collection of short stories, but it is going very slowly. It is possible that I could write something which has not been set in Ireland, but the speech rhythms of the place are the ones that are in my head.

TBR: Not one of your stories or novels has what might be called a "happy ending." Your characters seem doomed to lives of despair; as Cal remarks, "To suffer for something which didn't exist, that was like Ireland." For a writer who is faithful to his material, are happy endings possible when writing of Ireland? Is a happy ending to the "Irish question," to the Troubles, at all possible?

BML: A solution has got to come. I can imagine reading the history books in 2050 and seeing that a compromise was finally reached and people in Ireland stopped killing each other. If you are writing fiction out of the present context, then it is difficult not to reflect the pessimism. But what is wrong with that? I agree with Flannery O'Connor when she defends the right of the artist to examine the black side of things.

TBR: It has become a commonplace here that writers no longer matter in the daily life of American culture. Do writers matter in modern Irish life, in Irish politics? What can Irish writers do to serve their people best?

BML: No, writers do not matter. When I was at Cannes, a French interviewer asked me if I thought that the film *Cal* would help solve the Irish problem. I find that kind of naiveté laughable. There is a piece of graffiti on a wall outside Belfast which says, "If you are not confused you don't understand the situation." The best thing Irish writers can do is to write well.

A HANDLIST OF BOOKS BY BERNARD MAC LAVERTY

A Man In Search of a Pet (Blackstaff Press [Belfast], 1978)
Lamb (George Braziller, 1980)
Cal (Braziller, 1983)
A Time to Dance & Other Stories (Braziller, 1985)
Secrets & Other Stories (Braziller, 1985)
The Great Profundo & Other Stories (Grove Press, 1988)

• Literature and Family •

An Interview with Margaret Drabble

Carol Caine London

Margaret Drabble appears on the surface to be a paragon of old-fashioned femininity, with her conservative manner and flowery dresses, but she speaks with the strength, confidence, and learning of one who has found an independent voice through a substantial body of work. She has written nine novels, a scholarly biography of the Victorian writer Arnold Bennett, and the latest edition of a standard literary reference work, *The Oxford Companion to English Literature,* and she has edited the work of Jane Austen. Drabble had just left Cambridge University, having studied literature and criticism, when her first novel, *A Summer Bird-Cage,* was published in 1968. When her novel *Realms of Gold* was published in 1976, she was the mother of three children, had married and divorced actor Clive Swift, had acted with the Royal Shakespeare Company, and had established herself as one of England's leading contemporary writers. This interview was conducted in New York in the spring of 1985.

The Bloomsbury Review: How did you begin your career as a writer?

Margaret Drabble: My sisters and I used to do things like family magazines and Christmas plays, but I stopped writing for a long patch during my last years of schooling. I wrote very little while I was at Cambridge, because everything I wrote seemed so bad. I started writing seriously when I left university. Somehow the atmosphere there was highly critical and literary and didn't encourage creative writing. There was no reason why it should have. The emphasis was on scholarship, and I found it suppressive. As soon as I left, I started to write my first book, *A Summer Bird-Cage.*

When I finally sent it off to the publisher, I was completely on my own. I just sent it off out of the blue, as it were, with very little expectation that anyone would be interested in it. Nobody I knew then was writing. I think a lot of my friends were very surprised by the kind of book I'd written, in fact, because I was a very intense person at the university and worked very hard. *A Summer Bird-Cage* was very lighthearted.

The same fortnight I left university at age twenty-one I married Clive Swift, the actor. Acting was my first career choice. Writing was secondary.

TBR: You wrote under your maiden name.

MD: I always resented the idea that women had to give up their maiden names in marriage. It seemed rather silly. I was quite fond of my maiden name because it was rather eccentric. I think it's lovely having another name to disappear into, though, when you feel like it.

TBR: Your novels are much involved with children.

MD: Yes. During the years I was home with babies, it was hard for me to imagine a different kind of life. I write very much out of life as I see it developing around me, and those early books are so much of the fulfillment of children because that was my fulfillment. I was astonished that this should be so, because I had never thought that I would find such a life in any way satisfactory. When I was a teenager, I felt some distaste about having children. My mother, you see, a teacher of English literature, never got around to writing, but I think she harbored a secret desire to do so. She was always bringing up children, and then the war intervened. I think she felt quite envious of our having the freedom to do the things she was never able to do. But she was very encouraging about our work. My older sister is a writer; my youngest, an artist. I wrote my first three books while I was expecting my first three babies. Each took almost nine months. I remember that the proofs of *The Millstone* arrived while I was in hospital having Joseph. I must have written that book almost entirely while I was expecting him.

TBR: You didn't remain married.

MD: I think it's the children who made it a big strain rather than the two egos. Two egos are perfectly compatible so long as people can go away from each other and lead separate lives and then come back together. But with children, there's a need to maintain a home and a home life. It was extremely difficult. We parted, as they say, on the best of terms.

TBR: Does your writing come easily to you?

MD: Invariably I feel anxious. Even if it's only a short article where I know exactly what I am going to say, I feel this slight anxiety that it's not going to work and that I'm going to have a complete seizure and am going to be unable to do it at all. With a novel, I begin to feel anxious when it's halfway through. In the middle of the book, I wonder whether to plough on or to scrap it. That's happened with every book I've ever written.

TBR: Your work has often been compared to that of Doris Lessing.

MD: I had a long letter from someone in the States making that comparison once and saying that I wrote very elegantly and that she wrote very clumsily. But I think the upshot of it was that Lessing was much better than I. She is. I don't like all of her books, but I think she is a marvelous writer, and I don't think that what I am doing is comparable to what she has been doing. I can't think of anyone who has written such criticism at length, but then I don't read much criticism about myself. It usually annoys me.

TBR: Lessing's women espouse freedom from men, where your books are about close relationships with men and with children.

MD: I think I know why she does this. She became a Marxist, I think, because some of the communists she knew were very keen on getting rid of the family. She didn't get on with her own mother and father. It was as simple as that. I think that she would now say that some of that feeling has changed or has been evicted. I feel that this is what is most interesting about her. The women seem to want to get rid of the men. They want to be free, but in *The Four-Gated City,* which is a great book, Martha ends up as a kind of mother to the whole household, and she fulfills her maternal role in that lot, not one of them her own — other people's children, other husbands, and so on. I think that is something Doris admires. It's also something I admire.

TBR: Do you think of yourself as a traditionalist when it comes to family?

MD: I get uneasy when people occasionally do try to set me up as a supporter of the old-fashioned family, which I am not. In personal terms, I've been very much luckier in my domestic situation than Doris was. She had trouble with leaving the country and starting off again. I got on better with my parents than she did. I think the crucial difference between her books and mine is that in her work, people tend to leave their children, and in mine, this would be inconceivable. That doesn't mean that husband and wife should stick together through thick and thin. My own life bears witness to this.

TBR: The protagonist in *The Millstone* is passive until she has a child. Then she becomes quite courageous. Is she an autobiographical character?

MD: I used to endure any discomfort rather than cause offense. I would freeze to death in an underheated room, say. Having the baby, I wasn't as withdrawn and unable to cope and unwilling to assert myself. Having a baby makes you responsible for another person. I think I was trying to describe the process of becoming very much more human, in a realistic way.

TBR: And the protagonist in *The Garrick Year?*

MD: No. But the background is exactly what I was living in at the time. I was in the Royal Shakespeare Company. This was my most lighthearted book, really. It's quite funny, in a way. What I had done was to take the situation of being a Stratford-on-Avon wife. There were so many of them, having such a raw deal, really. I was having a better time, because I was in the theatre company too. Actors want to talk about the theatre all the time, and the book was sort of a double-edged revenge on them all for being so absurd.

TBR: In *Jerusalem the Golden,* I was moved by your having captured so beautifully the love for a baby. Yet you inserted that special baby while eliminating Gabriel, the only man to have truly loved Claire, your protagonist. Why was that?

MD: I remember putting that baby in because I'd realized there wasn't a baby anywhere else in the book. It crept in just because I wanted to describe it, I think. Claire is so unloved, she can't imagine loving, and it's turned her rather hard. She doesn't want to be dependent upon love. It won't work. She is somebody who is going to grow up to be a very hard person, I think. Claire is one of those modern people who would have been efficient about contraception. In my novel *The Ice Age,* her character reappears as a documentary filmmaker, unmarried and very successful.

TBR: You avoid straightforward depictions of sex until *The Waterfall,* with the scene in which the new mother, having just been deserted by her husband, makes love with her husband's cousin in a bed still bearing the stains of childbirth. Why did you create that scene?

MD: I'd been haunted for years by that first scene of the man and the baby, and I wanted to write it a long time before I finally did. I wrote it as a kind of self-contained chant. I think it's probably the best thing I've written. I like it best of anything I've written, that is, as a piece of what I've felt at the time. I find it difficult to write about sexuality at all, having been brought up as a nice, polite English girl.

TBR: *The Waterfall* is your favorite book, then?

MD: It's my favorite, although I consider *The Needle's Eye* the best written of my books. *The Waterfall* is a woman's book. It's about sexuality and being a woman, and it has no external subject at all. Yet I think it has more about what I wanted to say than my other books.

TBR: Why the switch from domestic settings to *Realms of Gold,* in which the protagonist is an archaeologist working in Tunisia?

MD: I have a friend who is an archaeologist in North Africa, and it seemed like a very good idea. I had also been reading about Carthage. It all fitted together in a very satisfactory manner. But I'd never been to North Africa, and I had to go there to see what it looked like so that I could give some proper, vivid description. In a sense, I was behaving as my character would have behaved. I was more energetic and forceful than I usually am, also more callous — in many ways, rather a ruthless woman, getting her own way all the time. It was quite nice, being in her image. It made me go up to people in stations and say, "I want these tickets, and if you haven't got them I shall complain," which I'm not very good at doing.

There are four children in the book who appear only incidentally. One of the themes is, "What does a mother do when the children grow up and they don't need her so much?" Then, if she's lucky, she has a career. The first image in the book is about a mother octopus which dies when it gives birth. It has a million little babies, and then it just sits in the nest and dies while guarding them. Even if you give it food, it won't eat. It's programmed so that it's done its bit, and then it dies. My character sits there in her hotel room, not quite ready to die, even though her children seem quite capable of feeding themselves, and she's got another forty years to go.

TBR: I would expect that a person with your literary education would be engaged in writing scholarly work and articles and stories for the little, literary journals.

MD: Yes, everything in my background would have indicated that I would be an unreadable literary writer, so I'm much more anxious to claim that I am a popular writer. I think that is one of the nicest things that has happened to me. I am a literary writer, but by some stroke of amazing good luck, I also seem to have a reasonably sized audience, which means there are far more readers like me around than anyone thought there ever were. Some people accuse me of writing women's magazine stuff in the worst sense and popular books in the worst sense, but I really don't mind that, because the people who read women's magazines can also read my books, and that's fine.

A HANDLIST OF BOOKS BY MARGARET DRABBLE

The Needle's Eye (Knopf, 1972)
The Millstone (New American Library, 1973)
A Writer's Britain (Knopf, 1979)
For Queen and Country (Houghton Mifflin, 1979)
Realms of Gold (Bantam, 1982)
The Garrick Year (New American Library, 1984)
A Summer Bird-Cage (New American Library, 1985)
The Ice Age (New American Library, 1985)
The Oxford Companion to English Literature, Fifth Edition (Oxford University Press, 1985)
Arnold Bennett: A Biography (G.K. Hall, 1986)
The Radiant Way (Knopf, 1987)
Jerusalem the Golden (New American Library, 1987)

• Survival Skills •

An Interview with Farley Mowat

Robert W. Smith

Farley Mowat, the Canadian ethnologist, naturalist, historian, and writer, has led a remarkable life right from the start. According to his father, he was conceived "in a green canoe on the shores of Lake Ontario in the autumn of 1920." Author of twenty-eight books and perhaps the leading authority on survival in nature, he enables readers to see in their lives the irony and liveliness he sees in his.

In April of 1985, six months after this interview, Mowat was prevented by American officials from boarding a plane in Toronto bound for Los Angeles, where he was going to promote his book *Sea of Slaughter.* Like Gabriel García Márquez, Carlos Fuentes, and many other foreign authors, Mowat had run afoul of the Immigration and Naturalization Service's program to deny entry visas to some fifty thousand individuals (two thousand of them Canadian) who were thought to endanger the security of the United States. The INS defended its action by citing Mowat's several visits to the USSR in the 1960s and his once having threatened to fire his .22-calibre rifle at any Strategic Air Command bomber flying over his Canadian home. Refuting Camus's dictum, "Stupidity has a knack of getting its own way," the furor raised by media and public forced the INS to retreat and to offer Mowat a one-time visit on parole. He scornfully declined, saying he would only come if President Reagan himself apologized and had him flown on Air Force One to Los Angeles. If federal officers thought that stopping Mowat would deter publicity and quash sales of *Sea of Slaughter,* they were wrong. It had just the opposite effect: the furor spurred sales, quickly forcing the book into extra printings.

Mowat's energy, alert mind, and Rabelaisian wit convey powerful presence. Robert Smith spent an afternoon in Port Hope, Ontario, with Mowat, his writer-artist wife Claire, his two Newfoundland dogs, Lily and Tom, and a herring gull of indeterminate sex tentatively called Gil.

The Bloomsbury Review: How do you feel about yourself so far? Have you accomplished what you wanted to in your life and work?

Farley Mowat: I don't think I ever set out to accomplish anything in particular. In fact, my whole life has been lived by jumping from log to log. I never had any long-term plans. I suppose I wanted success, whatever that means, and the plaudits of my peers — but those were always minor things. What I really wanted to do was to cope adequately with immediate challenges. This led me into a lot of causes. I wanted to change things, or, more correctly, to restore conditions that had probably obtained at earlier times in connection with man, the other animals, and the communal world in which we all live. Change is a hideous word that seduces and destroys. Like progress, it's a two-edged sword. I don't think I ever wanted to change anything — only to restore. However, I've come to doubt the ability of the individual to alter the mass march of the lemmings toward the sea.

TBR: But you don't regret the anger, your emotional involvement.

FM: Hell no, I don't regret the effort a bit. And I don't feel embittered that I've failed to achieve those limited goals of restoration. I don't even feel any sense of failure. I simply recognize that it was impossible for an individual to do very much.

TBR: Growing up, who were your heroes?

FM: The person who influenced me most was Ernest Thompson Seton, the naturalist. Subconsciously, I follow in his footsteps, a thing I'm just beginning to realize. *Two Little Savages,* I think, was the single book turning on my light. I lived it and relived it many times. It's autobiography disguised as fiction, about Seton's adventures as a young boy going into the countryside in Ontario to live with some Irish settlers, where he comes in contact with the real world of Indians and animals. The book had a tremendous effect on me, perhaps because for the first time I understood as a youngster the glory of compassion for other animals. You could feel for them the way you could feel for yourself. It wasn't a deadly sin to feel this way about other animals. When I grew up, of course, people who had strong emotions for other animals were considered either funny in the head or biologically queer. It was almost indecent for a person to admit love for another animal. That's changed, thank God. Now it's permissible to feel exactly the same toward some other form of life as toward your own species.

TBR: So Seton sparked your interest. From him did you go on to other naturalists?

FM: No, I became a naturalist through direct contact. A great-uncle of mine, Frank Farley, who had gone out to Alberta in the 1870s and become a naturalist, was my mentor. But he learned the trade by attrition, by killing and collecting. He did naturalizing over the sights of a shotgun and had an enormous collection of bird eggs and skins. He and others would trade eggs and skins back and forth. And it led me into that kind of natural history, collecting eggs, birds, and butterflies. I might have gone on and become a professional biologist, but the Second World War turned me around. After experiencing first-hand the slaughter, there was no way I was going to return and continue butchering other forms of life. But it took me a while to phase out. In the summer of 1946, I jumped in a jeep, drove to

Saskatchewan, and picked up exactly where I had left off in 1939 — collecting birds, establishing ranges, and doing habitat studies by killing the animals. About halfway through the summer, I just got sick of the whole thing. I gave my shotgun away to an Indian kid and packed up all my gear and shipped it home. I kept on with the jeep, finishing up in northern Saskatchewan living with a bunch of Indians. This contact eventually lead me to the Arctic and the inland Eskimos, the Ihalmuit.

TBR: Will you write the story of your father, Angus?

FM: No, I will never write about Angus. We had a schizoid relationship. On the one hand I owe him a great deal; on the other, he could be very damaging. He was arrogant, very intellectual, and selfish, the kind of man who would shape your life for you whether you liked it or not. He was charming. Everyone worshipped the ground he walked on except my mother. I was sucked into this attitude too. I always thought it was betrayal on my part if I didn't do what he told me and if I didn't sing his praises to the skies. And it wasn't until after he died that I realized this strange dichotomy. He was determined that I would be a literary novelist. He himself had written two unsuccessful novels. One of the positive things he did for me was to introduce me to Joseph Conrad. *People of the Deer,* my first book, delighted him, though he regarded it as "just an apprenticeship for the greater novels you are going to write." I never wrote an adult novel. Toward the end of his life, when *A Whale for the Killing* was published, I sent him a copy. I was rather pleased with it; it was the sort of book that I wanted to write. The next weekend I went to see him, and he didn't mention it, pretending that it had never even happened. Indeed, it hadn't. In his eyes, I still hadn't written a novel. This may seem petty, but it's good to get it off my chest. That was his negative side.

On the positive, he brought me up in an ambiance where the written word was everything. He was a peripatetic librarian, moving continuously. In the 1920s and 1930s we anticipated the modern era in which nobody stays in one place for more than three or four years. No sooner did we put roots down in one place than my father would become librarian in another town. I became a wanderer, like it or not, detribalized, never belonging anywhere. As a result, I had to build my own world to assuage my need for self-belief. Undersized for my age, I couldn't become a great athlete, so I turned to nature.

TBR: Were you ever tempted to forgo writing for a business career?

FM: A publisher friend of my father once offered me a job — probably because of my father's position as director of Public Libraries more than my capabilities — but I had no difficulty declining the offer. Taking a salaried position, forfeiting freedom for an 8:30 to 5:30 job, never appealed to me. For me, freedom is my typewriter.

TBR: The Russians admire that great quality *vynoshlivost,* "lasting a thing out" or endurance. Your works seem more concerned with this quality than with the passion for adventure and success that draws so many writers. You present man in the northern latitudes as a surviving entity, his life in harmony with other species and the terrain rather than overcoming them.

FM: There is no gap between the species. Species is a stupid word, an arbitrary categorization invented by mankind.

TBR: That correction made, would you agree that your concern is with the quality of endurance rather than with success in exploration?

FM: Oh, yes. Most physical exploration is stupid stuff with about as much merit as jogging. Polar explorations are of that ilk, but I admire people like Dr. Frederick Cook. Admiral Peary was a machine driven by ambition, but Cook was more human, more perceptive. He was very alive and sensitive to what he saw. He never reached the Pole — neither of them did — but his journey is infinitely more interesting than Peary's. He lived as an Eskimo with two real Eskimos for an entire winter.

I admire the primitive in man. I don't use that word in its usual sense. I use it as perhaps the greatest accolade that can be paid to any human being — in touch, still bearing all of the good qualities in life, not yet perverted by the view modern man has come to have of himself. Civilization I have little use for. I think we began to go wrong when we became agrarians and discovered the magic of agriculture. We could stay in one place then and accumulate things, and once you do that you have something to defend or envy. Then you get competition and modern politics and war and everything that is wrong with our society.

TBR: In your writing, how important is memory?

FM: Very important. Not conscious memory so much as subconscious memory. For fifty years I've envied people who had instant and total recall. Mine was never very good. But subconscious memory is different — you can't deal with it on demand. Subconscious memory emerges in its own good time when you give it the right cue. I usually start a book with no plan. I begin to type and eventually, after one page, twenty pages, five chapters, or whatever of laborious effort, the little trap door in the back of my mind opens, and the subconscious starts to operate. That's when I begin to recover things that I had forgotten and could never recall consciously. I could never have recovered the better half of my memoir of World War II, *And No Birds Sang,* consciously. Initially, I simply copied, using *The Regiment* as a framework, waiting for the moment when the trap door would spring open. And then, when it did, bang! I was awake.

TBR: In reading that book, I smelled the cordite.

FM: Yes, the two smells that are indissolubly welded into my conscious memory are the smell of shattered human flesh and cordite. Bad combination. Perhaps that's one of the reasons I turned against hunting. Firing a shotgun, I get the dual impact of the two terrible stinks. I hunted as a sportsman, going out with my little shotgun and shooting partridges and ducks and whatever, and as a scientist. In those days, the pursuit of biology, which really should be called necrology, was the pursuit of death.

TBR: Audubon was great for that.

FM: That's right. The early biologists — and a good many current ones — were killers.

TBR: Killing is the theme of *Sea of Slaughter.*

FM: Yes. The book recreates the conditions of animate life on the Atlantic seaboard in the region from Cape Cod north to Quebec and mid-Labrador, from the first European contacts about 1500 to the present. I began with the idea of simply portraying a few extinctions, such as the passenger pigeon, the great auk, and so on, but as I got into the research I realized that reductions in animal populations, not just extinctions, was the real story. I set myself a five-year plan aiming to reconstruct the fabric of life as it existed in 1500 in this one area, which can be extrapolated to cover the whole continent. I found the most dreadful depletions. For instance, as late as 1780 in the Gulf of St. Lawrence, a quarter of a million walrus thrived. By a century later, they had been completely exterminated. We had polar bears living as far south as Nova Scotia. The great auk, perhaps as many as one hundred million of them, crowded the coasts until they were totally exterminated. In brief, the book describes how the entire biomass of mammals, birds, and fishes has been reduced in this region by ninty to ninty-five percent.

TBR: How did you handle this bloodbath artistically?

FM: I made myself an anonymous scribe rather than remain in the foreground as I have in most of my books. And I employed all sorts of devices — chiefly bringing back the people of the period — to sustain interest.

TBR: Which wild animal in the eastern seaboard region today is the toughest survivor?

FM: Probably the coyote, the only medium-sized mammal that has increased rather than lost ground since the Europeans came here. When they arrived, coyotes were restricted to the Great Plains, but they can now be found from Alaska to Mexico, from the Pacific to the Atlantic. The wolverine and badger and musk ox are tougher physically, but the coyote is the most successful at outwitting man's biocidal tendencies.

TBR: It is said that an animal does not know that it is going to die, whereas we humans do.

FM: Who knows what they know? I believe many species are aware of death, but they seem quite relaxed about it. It is not something they fear. They attempt to evade it only within certain limits. They don't cheat death, and they don't try to. Humans try to all the time. Because we're so scared of dying, we live in terror. Closer to nature than most of us, the Cree Indians put it something like this: "We live as long as we are living; after that there is nothing. So there is no need to worry." That's a positive rather than negative concept.

TBR: Besides Seton, which writers have influenced you?

FM: My reading has been extraordinarily catholic. As the child of a librarian, I had no restrictions on what I could read. Librarians used to get gifts of pornographic stuff from the booksellers, and I read them all. I read all of the Dr. Doolittle books. At one point I was reading them and Rabelais back to back. I've read so much, so widely and eclectically, that it would be impossible to pinpoint the high spots. But I've always liked the great romantics, poets like Rupert Brooke.

He wrote wonderful stuff, things like "The Little Dog's Day," one of the great poems of our time.

TBR: What do you read these days?

FM: I hopefully read whatever comes along. The reason I say "hopefully" is that I keep hoping for a good story. And I don't know if it's me or whether it's the stuff that's being published these days, but I'm finding fewer and fewer good stories. Perhaps it's only a function of age, but I get little pleasure from modern writing. Every now and then, though, I'll find a rousing story and will love it. I'm a storyteller, a saga man; that's where I live as a working person, and it's where I relax and get pleasure. So if I'm not told a good story, I get bored. I hate trivia. These days you get a whole novel about some unimportant aspect of human behavior. Who the hell cares? Maybe the person who writes it does, but why inflict it on me? I want a damn good yarn.

TBR: In *The Siberians* you wrote about your trips to the USSR without doing the obligatory turn of criticizing the Russians. Instead, you portrayed those you met in Siberia as wonderful characters who treated you extremely well.

FM: I didn't encounter any nasty people, although there were some around as there always are everywhere. Once we were with Yuri Rytkheu, a Chukchee writer, at some airport, and we were getting drunk, and the plane was twelve hours late as usual. There was one Russian who looked exactly like a New York newspaper caricature of a bad Russian in a fur coat, a VIP from Moscow. He suddenly bellowed for quiet. Everyone was intimidated except Yuri, who said, "The big chief is on the wrong side of the mountains. He's on our side, and we'll do what we please." So we just kept on partying. In Magadan we heard stories about the labor camps from people who had lived in them but who have chosen to remain on at the end of their terms, because they don't want to go back to

Moscow, west of the Urals, to European Russia, where life is tightly controlled and bureaucratic. The farther you go away from Moscow, the easier things are. They told us frankly that life in the camps had been touch and go. But it wasn't my business to write about that. What I wanted to write about was their treatment of the native peoples, the small nations of the north, contrasted with our treatment of our native peoples. I'm so goddamned appalled by the way in which we're constantly misrepresenting the Soviets, turning them into black devils. And this is not only unfair, it is extraordinarily dangerous, because if we make them hateable enough, we'll want to kill them.

TBR: How can Russia and the West find peace?

FM: Perhaps the only way is to find a common enemy. Some twenty-five years ago I read a story in the *Saturday Evening Post* which, though trivial, has stayed with me. In it, a pacifist ex-US Army general bounces radar transmissions off the moon, and the signals are received on Earth as signals from an alien power. This brings the Americans and the Russians together finally in fear of a common enemy. Juvenile, but it hits the nail on the head. If something like this doesn't happen, we will probably destroy each other and everything else at the same time.

TBR: It's sad when you contemplate the artistic and intellectual achievements of humans, how science has resolved so much mystery....

FM: What's so wonderful about dissolving mystery? I used to believe that scientific progress was the greatest virtue. But what good does it really do? Are we really better off? Does the fact that we can map the universe for fifty billion light years or whatever leave us better off than the ancient Greeks? Are we better men — better animals — for that? Are we better living beings than Eskimos who believe that the Northern Lights are as far out as space extends? The older I get, the less I trust the intellectual side of man and his "enquiring nature" and the more I rely on the instinctive and intuitive acceptance of mystery as an integral part of life.

TBR: Aside from the intellectual, will you grant that humans have often created the beautiful?

FM: It's in the eye of the beholder, the human beholder. What the hell is beauty? I find it difficult to convince myself that a painting of life is better, more beautiful, or more meaningful than reality. Real is real. In architecture, I used to think that the greatest things we ever did were things like Canterbury and Rheims. But are they? They certainly took an incredible amount of work and soaked up a lot of labor. And they are artistically impressive. But they can't compare with the Carlsbad Caverns. Simply put, I prefer nature to imitations of nature.

TBR: I don't know what your writing plans are down the road, but the book I want to see, the one I hope you'll write some day, is an autobiography.

FM: Yes, I have it in mind, if not in the typewriter. I've even got a title for it — *Born Naked.*

A HANDLIST OF BOOKS BY FARLEY MOWAT

Never Cry Wolf (Little Brown, 1963)
Grey Seas Under (Ballantine, 1976)
The Snow Walker (Bantam, 1977)
And No Birds Sang (Little Brown, 1980)
People of the Deer (Bantam, 1981)
A Whale for the Killing (Bantam, 1981)
My Discovery of America (Atlantic Monthly, 1985)
Sea of Slaughter (Bantam, 1986)
The Siberians (Bantam, 1987)
Woman of the Mists (Little Brown, 1987)

• Sustained Emotions •

An Interview with Alastair Reid

Ray Gonzalez

Alastair Reid is widely recognized as one of our best translators of Latin American literature and a fine poet in his own right. Through his efforts, English readers have gained access to some of the best work by Pablo Neruda, Jorge Luis Borges, Mario Vargas Llosa, and other important writers from Latin America. Perhaps Reid is able to sustain the emotion of the poetry because of his own sensitivity as a poet. One critic has said of *To Lighten My House,* Reid's first book, and *Weathering: New and Selected Poems,* "Reid's poems happen. They do not try to arrange their substance rigidly, but rather in a natural irregularity."

Reid was born in Whithorn, Scotland, in 1926 and received a master's degree from St. Andrews University. He has been visiting professor at various universities in the United States and Europe and has received two Guggenheim fellowships and a Columbia University fellowship in writing. He has been a contributing editor to *The New Yorker* for many years. Reid now lives in the Dominican Republic. As of October 1985, when this interview took place in Durango, Colorado, Reid had given up translating to devote more time to his own writing.

The Bloomsbury Review: Why have you decided to stop translating after all these years?

Alastair Reid: There are many reasons. One is that translating takes three times as long as writing. Octavio Paz says that all creation is translation, the wordless to the word. But, if there is an original piece of work, there must be respect for that original. Also, there is not much money in translating, and I have lived off my writing for thirty years. I also have many things I want to write. There are many fine young translators publishing in this country, which is rich with good translators. I must make room for them. I'm all for a variety of translators, because the one thing I detest in translators is when they claim the original as their property. This is the opposite of the way it should be. The more versions of the same poem there are, the better. Gregory Rabassa is a good example of a translator who never repeats himself, loves translating, and takes on new writers he has never done before. There are just too many translators who colonize a specific writer's work and keep others away. That shows a real meanness of spirit.

TBR: You have translated Pablo Neruda's work for many years. As you know, there are several different versions of the same poems in English. How do you think his work in English will be seen years from now?

AR: There are a great number of Neruda translators, but there are also many Pablo Nerudas. He was nine or ten poets in one. He went through many phases. He would shed one identity, like a snake shedding its skin, and start writing another kind of poetry. Different translators have found their own Nerudas.

The Neruda I translated is the one I knew well — in what he called his "atominal" period, when he settled down with his wife, Matilda, in Isla Negra. He left the odes behind and wrote very warm, human lyrics, from the book *Extravagaria* to the work in *Isla Negra*. These poems were so warm that they suited me as a translator and could be accommodated in English in a way *Machu Picchu* never could be. That is my Neruda. I knew him well, knew his home on Isla Negra.

TBR: How do you think all the different versions of Neruda affect the reader approaching his work?

AR: I think the whole is still greater than the sum of its translated parts. To read all of Neruda is a monumental undertaking, and, to be truthful, a lot of it is terrible. There is an untranslated book, *Las Uvas y el Viento* [*The Grapes and the Wind*], which is terrible, very uneven. Neruda wrote torrents of poetry, and a lot of it was bad but does contain jewels. It is worth learning Spanish to read the whole of Neruda. But for those readers who do not, translators let them peer over the edge of his work.

TBR: Would Neruda ever admit he wrote some bad poetry?

AR: Neruda would never admit that because no one would bring it up. He was always going on to newer work. He wrote so easily, like breathing. Sometimes after breakfast at Isla Negra he would rise, stretch, and say, "Now, I'm going to work." He would go and return from his study an hour and a half later. I would say, "So, you are not going to write today?" He would answer, "Oh, it is done. It is finished." He would fill his notebooks in a bright green ink he always used. He probably never saw the poems again until they turned up in proofs.

TBR: Is it true that there are volumes of his work still untranslated?

AR: Oh, yes. If you took Neruda's three thousand collected poems, they would barely scratch the surface.

TBR: What advice would you give future translators about approaching the enormous body of his work?

AR: You can't direct the translation of Neruda, even though I have advised some publishers on what to do. Jack Schmidt is doing a wonderful translation of *Canto General.* We need all of it in English.

Young translators of Neruda should translate out of passion and the need to do it. They should not be thinking about the need to publish their newest Neruda translation. The experience of translation is a magnificent immersion in the poem, to be able to move around in it, through it. That true experience takes years, and the end does not have to be publication.

TBR: How did you know which of Neruda's works to translate into English?

AR: I did not select from the large body of work. When I first met Neruda in 1964, he was working on the proofs of *Isla Negra* at his house on Isla Negra. I had no intention of translating them. But on one visit, he handed them to me, and I saw they were tremendous poems. I told him so, and he asked me to translate some of them, which I did out of enthusiasm. By coincidence, Jonathan Cape in London had gotten the rights to publish a volume of Neruda's work, so he asked me to do it. I went on to translate more work from that same period.

I read all of Neruda's work but never felt as close to other phases of it as I did to the books I translated. What also helped me is that Neruda loved *Extravagaria* and *Fully Empowered,* two books I did. They were two favorites of his, so he kept pushing me to translate them.

TBR: How did you become a translator?

AR: I had no intention of being a translator. I didn't learn Spanish until I was thirty. I went to Spain because it was cheap to live there and got pulled in by the Spanish language. I kept meeting Spanish writers and was ashamed that I couldn't communicate with them, so I learned the language and began to translate as an exercise to help my Spanish. I translated unknown Spanish poets. Then I had an Argentine girlfriend who told me our relationship would be nothing unless I learned Spanish well enough to read Borges to her in the original.

TBR: One of your last translations is *Legacies* by the Cuban poet Heberto Padilla. How did you approach his work as compared to Neruda's?

AR: There is no theory of translation possible, nor is translation of any use unless you think of it as an existential act. Every single work has different requirements for the translator. Every poem needs to be taken in its own right. Even separate poems in the same book raise different problems, regardless of what you have done up to that point. You forget everything, immerse yourself in the poem, and that is all there is. My approach to Padilla was fresh and new, just as my approach to Neruda was. Padilla's work was at hand. Forget Neruda. Just think of the poem that is before you.

TBR: Is it true that the poems in *Legacies* were smuggled out by friends of Padilla when he was in prison?

AR: He was under house arrest for nine years in Cuba. Friends of his connected with *The New York Review of Books* brought some of his poems out of the house and asked me to translate them.

TBR: Did knowing Padilla was restricted affect the way you approached his work?

AR: No, I did not feel that bringing his poems out endangered him, nor did I feel more passionate about them because of his political problems. I translated them because they were good poems I felt good about.

TBR: Fidel Castro punished Padilla for his political beliefs, and he was attacked by the international writing community for persecuting Padilla. As the one who translated his work, do you feel a special responsibility to his cause?

AR: Padilla has always wanted people to read his poems without thinking back to his political situation. He detests his notoriety because it keeps people from reading his poems just as poems. One of the most satisfying things is that we sat at a table and worked on the translations together. We were able to exchange ideas on the languages, the same way we did when he translated my work into Spanish. We were living the process of translation.

TBR: How did he decide to translate your poems?

AR: He read my poems, was very enthusiastic about them, and felt they should be translated into Spanish. He also translated a long prose memoir that I wrote.

TBR: You have done a lot of work besides translations. Many of your books of poems are hard to find today.

AR: Yes, that is the publishing game. But some are coming back into print. I have written more than twenty books. Nowadays, some publishers are bringing reprints back onto the market. A book of collected prose pieces, *Whereabouts,* will be out in 1986.

TBR: One of your most highly acclaimed translations is *Don't Ask Me How the Time Goes By,* by the Mexican poet José Emilio Pacheco. But when people talk about Mexican poetry, his name rarely comes up. Do you think Pacheco deserves more recognition?

AR: Yes. Mexican poets know him and recognize his work, and most will say Pacheco is the crucial influence in their work. His name has not circulated much in English. The one book I did was buried and didn't get much attention. Pacheco is an astute critic. He does not speak English very well, but he is a voracious reader of English. He is greatly admired as a critic in Mexico, and what he thinks filters down to other poets.

TBR: Many readers of international poetry depend on translators to find out what is going on in other countries. But sometimes outstanding writers like Pacheco are overlooked, while Gabriel García Márquez or Mario Vargas Llosa are noticed. Why are some writers picked over others who may be equally good?

AR: A lot of it is just luck, playing a lottery. You never know who is going to be popular and read one year and who will be in the next. Look at writers in the United States who rise to best-seller status, while better writers are unknown.

TBR: Is there anything you, as a translator, can do to get more people to notice writers like Pacheco?

AR: The most important thing is to translate them and make sure they get published. A translator does not have power in the business other than choosing who he translates. He can advise publishers, but not much more than that.

TBR: Do younger poets like Pacheco approach writing about Mexico in a different way than Paz does?

AR: Yes, they approach Mexico in as many different ways as there are Mexican intellectuals.

TBR: Over the years of doing translations, were you ever aware that the translating process affected your own poetry?

AR: No. I was never conscious of translating as my major task. What I would do is rise early and work on a book I was translating. I'd do that for a couple of hours and then go on to my own work. It was like going to the gym and working out. After two hours of translating, I was in shape to do my own writing. I never put aside my own writing for translation. Translating was work for the left hand; writing was work for the right hand.

TBR: What kind of writing are you doing now?

AR: I live in the Dominican Republic, about a quarter of a mile from where Christopher Columbus first landed in January of 1493. It is where the first Indian blood was shed in the New World. I have been reading a great deal about those first voyages of discovery to write something about finding the New World. I have also been working on short pieces of memoirs. And I have begun to write poems again, after swearing off poetry for seven years.

TBR: How do you feel looking back on the large body of translations you have done? When people mention translators, your name comes up as one who has brought a tremendous amount of important poetry into English.

AR: That is very gratifying, but I don't look at it that way. Someone once wrote an essay about Latin American writers and the friendship among them and how important that was. Translating has brought me many precious friendships with the writers. To me, the friendships are more important than the translations themselves. Talking and getting to know these writers helped my work as a translator immeasurably.

Closeness to the writer may not always be necessary for a translator, but it was very gratifying to send Pacheco my work on his poems and get a ten-page letter back scrutinizing what I had done. The same goes for working with Padilla across the desk, or with Cabrera Infante, who would change the original as we got going and made it all a lot of fun. Neruda was always very generous, and Borges was always interested in the process of translating. They kept translation from being confining, although I always wound up doing it myself. I got to feel the wavelength from these writers by talking to them. I translated out of exuberance, not out of obligation. I have had a very lucky life as a translator.

A HANDLIST OF BOOKS BY ALASTAIR REID

To Lighten My House (Morgan, 1953)
Oddments Inklings Omens Moments (Little Brown, 1959)
Passwords: Places Poems Preoccupations (Little Brown, 1963)
Weathering: New and Selected Poems (Dutton, 1978)
Whereabouts: Notes on Being a Foreigner (North Point, 1987)

Translations

Ficciones by Jorge Luis Borges (Grove, 1965)
We Are Many by Pablo Neruda (Grossman, 1968)
Jorge Luis Borges: A Personal Anthology (Grove, 1967)
with Ben Belitt, *A New Decade: Poems 1958-67*
by Pablo Neruda (Grove, 1968)
Selected Poems by Pablo Neruda (Delacorte, 1972)
Extravagaria by Pablo Neruda (Farrar, Straus & Giroux, 1974)
Sunday, Sunday by Mario Vargas Llosa (Bobbs-Merrill, 1973)
Fully Empowered by Pablo Neruda (Farrar, Straus & Giroux, 1976)
Don't Ask Me How the Time Goes By by José Emilio Pacheco
(Columbia University Press, 1977)
Isla Negra by Pablo Neruda (Farrar, Straus & Giroux, 1981)
Legacies by Heberto Padilla (Farrar, Straus & Giroux, 1982)

• Armed Visions •

An Interview with John Nichols

John Sullivan & Ray Gonzalez

In the summer of 1968, a young John Nichols, flush with the success of his first published novel, *The Sterile Cuckoo,* moved from his home in New York City to the arid expanses of northern New Mexico. When Nichols arrived, he was full of the hyperidealism of his youth, charged with a zeal to inform America about capitalism and its ill effects on the modern world, including the little patch of earth he lived on — Taos, a small town north of Sante Fe. Twenty years later, Nichols is well settled in his small universe. While he maintains that his political ideology has remained constant over the years, Taos itself has changed. The materialism Nichols so regrets has firmly established itself, in the form of a neon-and-fast-food strip into town and a score of subdivision developments that cater to those seeking an "alternative" way of life, a contrived wonderland of nature and controlled existence.

Nichols has stayed on among them, writing his books and extending his political views to those who will listen. Although he admits to being a polemicist, Nichols is affable and gregarious. He has attained the success most important writers come to know, yet acquired none of the taste for artifice and eccentricity that seems to be a part of the bargain. He is, for all the acclaim surrounding him and his work, an unaffected, straightforward man.

John Sullivan interviewed Nichols in Taos in the summer of 1981.

The Bloomsbury Review: In *Nirvana Blues,* you seem to take a sympathetic view of the Anglo transplants who have infested Chamisaville. Why? Have you had a change of heart toward these people?

John Nichols: It's odd you should say sympathetic. The people who've read it so far seem to think I have a nihilistic point of view toward the entire society. I've always looked at Chamisaville as infinity in a grain of sand, as a microcosm of our country. The people from *The Milagro Beanfield War* through *The Magic Journey* to *Nirvana Blues* represent to me American society at a particular point in time. *Nirvana* is just a book I wrote about bourgeois culture, middle-class white people. My great fear in writing the book was that, because I had essentially an underlying lack of sympathy for me-oriented people, the narcissism of human-potential groups, human-awareness cults, gurus, EST, Eckankar — all of that stuff — I would write a mean and vicious satire. I didn't want to do that because I thought that even if you're writing about your enemies, you should have compassion toward them, and that made me very nervous about the book.

TBR: How do you field criticism that your characters are so overdone and preposterous as to amount to stereotypes, caricatures?

JN: I think there's a strong feeling, particularly in literary criticism, that you're supposed to expend most of your energy on problems inherent in developing characters. In most of the work I've written, what's interested me a lot more is the particular social situation and the dynamic of that situation, so that to me, in both *The Milagro Beanfield War* and *The Magic Journey,* the most important thing — the main character, so to speak — is the interaction, the class struggles between the individuals at various levels in this little town. The characters have been, in a sense, secondary. I've seen each character as a particular molecule that fits into the overall scheme.

TBR: The word "molecule" is interesting. That's perhaps why you're able to create so many characters, since you look at them as small parts that go into making up a broad picture.

JN: Sure. I'm not in it to do these great character studies. Curious, though, how some people will make that criticism while other people will go out of their way to say they're amazed I develop so many characters that seem real to them. The characters seem to have pretty universal applications; people identify easily with them. For example, you live in a small town like Taos or a small state like New Mexico, everyone wants to consider these books *romans-à-clef,* books that use actual characters in them. So people are always coming up to me, whether they're in Santa Fe or Taos or Questa or El Rito or Ojo Caliente or Alamosa or San Luis, and saying, "When did you live in Alamosa? I recognize that VISTA volunteer. We had a VISTA volunteer just like that." And the people in San Luis say "When did you ever live in San Luis? We have a José Mondragón!" People do this all over the Southwest. I get letters now from all over the country where people pretty much identify with the characters and the situation, but it's always tied into the situation.

TBR: Are characters like Amarante Cordova and Eloy Irribarren realistic, or have you romanticized them in order to make your point?

JN: Is Picasso's painting realistic? Are Diego Rivera's characters realistic? I think my books are very realistic and I think they're pretty accurate about what goes down in society, the whole mood and nature of our culture. But there's a lot of mythology, surreal stuff, exaggerations, caricatures, and things that go into making up the mood of these books, which isn't exactly realistic. You know, Hieronymus Bosch isn't realistic and yet there's something very real about the mood of these paintings — you learn something very real about the culture and attitudes of that particular time. No, I'm not sitting down trying to write James T. Farrell at all. That's not my goal. My feeling is if there's a total cultural accuracy in the books, it's good. Everybody tells their truth through their own particular style. I'm not sure that writers should spend much time analyzing their own shit. There are other people who can usually do that a lot better than they can.

TBR: In reading *The Nirvana Blues,* one can't help noticing a different style of humor from that of *The Milagro Beanfield War.* Have you become more cynical?

JN: No, I think *Nirvana* is probably more lighthearted than *Magic Journey,* which paints a pretty dark picture of struggle and cultural genocide and how capitalism functions. During the sixties I wrote a lot of novels that were just nihilistic. I never published any of them. When I wrote *Milagro,* I decided I needed to try and survive as a writer and I figured that if I wanted to get my polemics out I'd have to find another way of doing it. I was just being hard-assed, you know, writing books that were up-against-the-wall-honky-mother-fucker-black-power's-gonna-get-your-mama. So I bent over backwards to be humorous and it worked. It was a lot of fun.

Milagro is a book with a lot of flaws. One of them was that it was impossible, having set the tone for it, to also really get into how heavy it can be to be impoverished, or to be a victim, to be a minority in this country. Which is why I wanted to write *Journey* — to make sure there were no bones about understanding what the darker side can be like. *Nirvana* is, I suppose, a combination of both those things. I don't have a lot of sympathy for the whole middle-class bourgeois capitalistic culture. And I think that shows through in all my books. I'm not a working-class revolutionary. I'm a middle-class writer. But we all have dreams and sensibilities and we all have a particular vision of what it takes to have the planet survive. It's hard because I believe I have a lot of hope for the future. And I think a lot of that comes from a political point of view that believes you can work with the present, you can change nihilistic tendencies, you can change through struggle. Back in the sixties I was sort of an emblem of our culture, you know, a success story. I used to think nothing was better than America. Then I got turned around during the Vietnam War. I relearned American history, blew away my old foundations, and started recreating a belief system on a whole different level. It was very hard, rejecting most of the things that I really accepted wholeheartedly growing up. When I watch most of my old friends, or most of middle-class America, I see a real despair and cynicism and self-absorption, a kind of selfishness that gets translated into a lack of fulfillment. Everybody's desperate to be fulfilled and so many people are just locked into selfish pursuits. That's capitalism, it's based on selfishness and what's known as creative alienation — you've got to be able to keep people separated from each other in order to be competing with each other. One of the problems with *Nirvana* is that in the end you get left without a whole hell of a lot of hope for the future.

TBR: You seem to have a real sympathy for characters like Joe Mondragón in *Milagro* and Joe Miniver in *Nirvana.* Is that because these characters are, more or less, your own personality rising to the surface through your writing?

JN: All characters are your own personality rising to the surface. My brother called me up after reading *Milagro* and said he got a kick out of it because there were two hundred and fifty people, all of whom were myself. I found in my life that the closer I got to writing books that were really me, all of them were self-conscious books. Because I've never been able to write a book that gets really close to my own personality, even though all the books that you write are really close to your own personality. With *The Sterile Cuckoo* I very self-consciously split up my own personality and each part was one of the major characters in that book. But in *Milagro,* after the first draft, I had one of the characters as a writer and his wife living in this little town and they were the only characters that didn't work; it was just too damn self-conscious, so I cut them out. Most of my writing is intuitive and instinctive. I don't explain myself a whole lot — why I'm doing what I'm doing. I may start an eight hundred page book on a one-sentence premise. I don't plan things out, I don't really know where they're going to go. I follow it where it takes me and I write things that people can interpret in a lot of ways. And my writing is autobiographical to the extent that everything you do is. Any writer who says his writing isn't autobiographical is full of shit. Having gotten that out of the way, *Nirvana* is not more autobiographical than any other book I've written.

TBR: With each book in your New Mexico trilogy, your writing style seems to change. In *Nirvana,* your sentences seem much richer and complex, your images more direct and telling. How do you account for the different, changing styles?

JN: I haven't gone back over them to observe the change — I don't know if I've grown as a stylist. I've often felt that the most artistic book I've written was *The Sterile Cuckoo,* even though I wrote it when I was twenty-three years old. I struggled harder on style with that particular book than I ever struggled on style since. I was extraordinarily self-conscious about art. I was extremely absorbed with people like F. Scott Fitzgerald and Hemingway. I wanted to write things tight and with sentences that flowed in special ways. I wasn't as absorbed in the content as I was in the style. In the following years, I've become more absorbed in the content than in the style. Yet at the same time, the style is probably going to grow. One thing that happens is you set a tone when you're writing a book, you set a tone given the material, and the material will often dictate a style.

Nirvana is interesting because it's probably the closest to a first-person narrative that I've written. Whereas in *Milagro* and *Journey,* I could jump around to all different characters. One chapter would be Joe Mondragón, the next would be Ladd Devine, the next would be Horsey Shorty. In *Nirvana,* Joe Miniver's always on stage. It's the closest I've come to a first-person epic. And that dictates a different style. *Nirvana* also takes place in seven days, so there's a lot of writing about very small things. Whereas in *Journey,* one chapter covers five years. And there's a whole different kind of expression that's used to do that.

TBR: Describe your writing process.

JN: I'm real haphazard. What I do is, most importantly, try to get the first draft. In order to get the first draft, I sit down and make sure I do ten or twenty pages a day just to keep momentum. I'm not interested at all in whether or not it gels, I don't give a shit about the writing — all I want is movement and motion. I want to throw in all the material I can, whatever comes to mind, just get some kind of monster, a block of paper that I can work on. So I get ten or twenty pages a day that I can work on religiously, every day, till I get a first draft. It usually takes from one to five months. Then, after that, I work very haphazardly. Sometimes I work an eight-hour day, sometimes I work for three hours or three days, sometimes an hour a day for three paragraphs. I'll carry a manuscript in the car with me and sometimes just pull off the road if I have an inspiration and work on two or three pages. What's most important to me is to get the thrust of the story and worry about the writing later. I'd just die if I did it sentence by sentence — if I had to have one good sentence before I started the next, I think I'd lose complete track of the momentum of the story, and the flow. I write with my ear, not with my head. I often will write sentences that have almost no meaning at all, but I like the words and the sound — the noise that they make feels right with the mood of what I'm working on. I don't have much intellectual or literary discipline. I have a lot of discipline when it comes to hard work. I'm willing to rewrite and rewrite and rewrite. So, I go through various drafts until I start getting it honed down to where I think it will work. I have a rule that every time I start a book, I always go through to the complete, clean first draft, which means that I do a rough first, rewrite, retype it. But I never stop a book part of the way through. I'd stop everything I ever wrote because I usually hate what I'm working on as soon as I get into it a little. The final step is, when I've got the story down and when I've got the structure the way I want it to be, to write it. I have a theory about the craft. I have particular prejudices about not repeating certain words and mixing up sentence structure. That's when you sit there with a thesaurus and try to recall three or four synonyms for the word "gentle" or the concept of being misty. Once I do that then the manuscript is pretty much finished. And that usually takes me a lot longer to do than the other writing of the book. But I care about that a lot. Many people accuse my writing of being very loose and sort of sloppy, which may be true. But, you know, everybody has extraordinary amounts of flaws, from Dostoyevsky to Sidney Sheldon. Basically, all I can do is write stuff that sounds okay to me. I suppose every writer has his own indulgence. It may be a real indulgence to write an eight hundred page manuscript instead of doing it in three hundred.

TBR: In an interview in 1978, you said that you often tried to merge your own politics with your writing in order to develop a polemic art, like Upton Sinclair or Carl Sandburg. Do you feel that you've successfully merged the two in *The Nirvana Blues?*

JN: "Armed creativity," we call it.... I hope I've achieved it in *Nirvana*. It's not as overt as *Journey,* which people often critique for being so openly polemical. What they mean is left-wing Marxist polemical. *Nirvana* isn't as polemical because that wasn't the point. I certainly haven't changed my politics, they just seem to get stronger. I'm not planning to write books that are openly shouting out that this is a Marxist-manifesto person writing. My perspective hasn't changed in the last fifteen years or so, and my politics have been fairly consistent in the trilogy. But I don't have to repeat.

TBR: Each year northern New Mexico seems more crowded, more built up, more "pizzafied," as you would say. Does this affect your conviction to stay in New Mexico? Do you suppose you'll move?

JN: Where are you going to go? New Mexico is in the United States in the same system that governs the United States. You can't run any place and have it be different. So, as far as I'm concerned, I'm staying in New Mexico. If I went to New York City it would be the same as if I went to upstate Vermont which would be the same as if I went to Telluride, Colorado, which would be the same as if I went to Eugene, Oregon.

TBR: What do you plan to write next?

JN: I've just finished a nonfiction book called *The Last Beautiful Days of Autumn*. The next novel I'd like to write is an enormous novel about the rise of industrial capitalism in our country, from about 1865 to the present. I've got a library of about two hundred and fifty research books with everything from Ida Tarbell's *History of Standard Oil* to biographies of Lucy Parsons, everything I can get my hands on. I have a feeling this next project is going to be seven or eight years of work. But I feel that to do another major novel on the area in which I live would be repetitive. I feel I've tapped that major vision and now I want to do something else — that new project that's always there broiling in my head.

John Nichols did not sit still after *The Bloomsbury Review* interviewed him in 1981. He continued to write and speak out against American government policies and the destruction of the western United States, both of which, he believes, will eventually lead to the destruction of our planet.

In those years, too, Nichols wrote *American Blood,* a novel that continues to cause much controversy among both critics and readers. *American Blood* recounts the odyssey of Michael Smith, a veteran of the war in Vietnam, as he searches for peace within the violence of American society. Of the book, Nichols has said, "I am convinced that despair is the worst betrayal, the coldest seduction, to believe at last that the enemy will prevail." In the end, Nichols's characters prevail, just as they did in his New Mexico trilogy.

Nichols was interviewed in May of 1987 by Ray Gonzalez at the offices of *The Bloomsbury Review.*

The Bloomsbury Review: *American Blood* is an indictment of the Vietnam War and what it did to this country. Why is it appearing now, years after the war ended?

John Nichols: I don't see it as an indictment of the Vietnam War but as an indictment of our country, which has used violence in its foreign policy since the days of the Pilgrims. The book is not so much about Vietnam as it is about violence in our culture. Vietnam is the most graphic metaphor we have had in the last twenty years to describe the history of our culture. I did not intend this novel to be part of the Vietnam memorabilia but an attempt to wake people up to the dehumanizing effect of our country's daily existence. Vietnam was a continuation of our national character, one that goes back several hundred years. Genocide of Native Americans and the killing of the buffalo can be placed alongside Vietnam. It was official government policy to wipe out the buffalo and starve Native

Americans into proving what General Phil Sheridan said: "The only good Indian is a dead Indian." We did the same thing in Vietnam and the Philippines.

TBR: Response to *American Blood* is bound to be influenced by the response to the movie *Platoon* and the fact that there is a national reevaluation of Vietnam now afoot. The intense honesty of the novel is upsetting to some: Tom Clark, writing in *The Denver Post,* called you a "bleeding-heart liberal who had gone overboard." How do you respond to that kind of criticism?

JN: I don't really know how to respond to criticism because people critique a book from a million different angles. Some people call you the greatest genius since Charles Dickens, and some call you the greatest idiot since Max Schulman. There seems to be some confusion over the novel, as is indicated by the mixed reviews it has gotten. No one has explained it the way I would, but writers shouldn't explain their books. Others can do it better. Still, you can get your dander up at being called a bleeding-heart liberal.

TBR: The first thirty pages of the novel are the most violent and graphic and the hardest to get through. How did you feel after you wrote them? Do you have any regrets about starting the book that way?

JN: Lousy! Actually, it was instinct to start graphically instead of just talking about Michael Smith's behavior. I chose the flashbacks but thought, "My God! People are going to be vomiting by page ten and won't finish the book!" I had a book of photographs of World War I veterans who had been wounded. Many had eyes and parts of their faces missing, and they were horrible to look at. But the intolerable images of what war does brought the message home. We play around too much, censor ourselves too much when it comes to what we do to get the message across. As a democracy, we pretend that our luxury is obtained without harm to other human beings. We don't think about the fact that beautiful, spic-and-span downtown Denver got its skyscrapers by tormenting the earth. People died in quarries and sweatshops and the Hopi were displaced by coal companies so cities like Denver could be built. We slough off a lot in our society, and those first thirty pages of the book say that we cannot slough off what we did in Vietnam. As a writer, you learn certain rules about what is palatable and what isn't, and you wind up censoring yourself to fit the rules. Not everyone is a Dalton Trumbo who can write *Johnny Got His Gun* and make it effective. I've gone out on a limb with this book.

TBR: *American Blood* is very different from your other novels. Did you have a different audience in mind when you wrote it?

JN: No, except that the audience should be universal. Ideally, a writer wants everyone to read him. I don't know what the range is of the people who read my books. A large number must be fairly political and radical. At the same time, little old ladies in Wichita, Kansas, are reading books like *When Mountains Die* and *On the Mesa.* Some are environmentalists in the Wendell Berry-Edward Abbey mode. I know for a fact that others are fairly conservative, people who drive Winnebagos through our national parks and are touched by the lyrical tone of nature writing. I would like the same people who enjoyed *On the Mesa* to read *American Blood.*

TBR: Is the character of Michael Smith based on someone you know?

JN: He is a universal person who is angry and crippled by the violence of Vietnam and our society, even though it doesn't take Vietnam to bring out all the violence in this country. I don't want his character or the novel to be isolated as just a Vietnam novel. It was our culture that created Vietnam, just as it is creating the whole Contra thing in Nicaragua.

TBR: The novel is violent, fast-paced, psychedelic, and dark, but in the end Michael Smith breaks out of the darkness to start his life over. What were you aiming at with such a hopeful ending?

JN: I wanted to show that it is possible to survive the holocausts of our time. Many books and movies about Vietnam seem to end hopelessly, but *American Blood* is about survival and overcoming all those things. We live in a nihilistic society where it is fashionable not to hope. Eat, drink, and be merry! Our economic system has trained us to be selfish and to look out for ourselves without developing a social conscience. How many of us really think about our limited resources? If we speak out on this issue or suggest that our system of consumption needs to be changed, we become enemies of the state. If we write something against policy, we become enemies of the state, just like everyone who spoke out against the Vietnam War. Why is the Reagan administration so upset over Nicaragua? A country of two million people can't harm us, but it has become a metaphor for protecting our business interests down there. The same for El Salvador, Guatemala, Honduras, and any other country we exploit.

TBR: In your essay, "The Writer as Revolutionary," you say your writing is overtly political, what you call advocacy literature. Isn't that a high risk for a writer in the West? People want to read about lovely landscapes and western Americana.

JN: You have to talk about the political struggle, or there won't be any beautiful landscapes for people to read about. People in the West need to take a more active role in preserving this part of the country.

I truly believe there is no such thing as an apolitical person. Everyone has a stance. There is no such thing as an apolitical work of art. To me, literature is the most political tool there is. In one of his poems, Brecht says, "Young man, reach for a book. It is a weapon." I consider my writing active, political work.

TBR: You also state in the essay that you are committed to working for the defense of the Southwest. Are you still fighting political battles in New Mexico?

JN: Yes, but my defense of the Southwest has universal implications, whether I'm attending town meetings in Taos or fighting to control river rafting on the wild stretches of the Rio Grande. It is also connected to putting up the money to send your son on a work brigade in Nicaragua or helping with a benefit to fight radioactive dumping in southern New Mexico. John Muir said that when you pick out one part of something, you find it is always connected to the whole.

TBR: What kinds of creative projects are you working on now?

JN: I'm working on a six-hour television mini-series about Pancho Villa. Theoretically, it is slated for prime-time television and is being funded by CBS and produced independently by the people who did *Tender Mercies.* I'm not sure if my point of view will be able to get on prime-time television. This is the kind of project that, with luck, skill, ingenuity, and Machiavellian manipulation, will teach Americans a little more about a Third World country like Mexico. There is an extraordinary complexity to Pancho Villa and the Mexican revolution. I want to elevate him beyond the stupid, preconceived idea in this country that he was just a fat Mexican bandit. What I would like to do in six hours is to give people a lesson on how American imperialism affects Third World countries — specifically, how the United States, under Taft and Wilson, manipulated the Mexican revolution. If I can get the show on American TV, it will be a miracle. The chances are that somewhere down the pike I will be fired. Every now and then, something gets through, though. When I was working on *Missing* for Costa-Gavras, people thought the picture would never be made because it was too anti-American. In the final analysis, I wish it had been more political, but it did get through.

TBR: What is the latest news on Robert Redford's filming of *The Milagro Beanfield War?*

JN: The film is in the can, and Redford is editing it at Sundance in Utah. It is scheduled for release at the end of October. During the course of the filming, a group of Hispanic producers who had been working on a film of the life of Reyes Tijerina, the great activist in New Mexico, threatened to sue Redford. Moctezuma Esparza, the filmmaker, and David Ward, the screenwriter, claimed that Redford's film was undermining their efforts to make *King Tiger,* the story of Tijerina. They claimed that *Milagro* is based on his life and that Columbia Pictures pulled out when they found out Redford was making his film. The idea that I based *Milagro* on Tijerina's life is absurd, but the story made all the papers. They issued press releases saying they were suing Redford, but they never filed a suit because Tijerina pulled out of it. He didn't want anything to do with the suit. One other controversy was when they wanted to shoot the film in Chimayo, north of Santa Fe, because the village has a beautiful plaza that would have been perfect. The people of Chimayo felt it would be too much of an intrusion to have a film company there, so Redford pulled out. They had already started building sets because most of the people did want them, but the more radical citizens won. So they did the filming in the town of Truchas, which is near Chimayo.

TBR: Do you ever feel like putting *The Milagro Beanfield War* behind you and going on? Obviously, it is your most famous book, and the film will certainly make it known beyond the readership it already has.

JN: Yes, but for ten years hardly anyone paid attention to the book, except for the dedicated masochists who love it and read it over and over. On one level, I put it behind me when I moved to the next book. At the same time, books have a life of their own. I hope the political message lives with the life of the book.

A HANDLIST OF BOOKS BY JOHN NICHOLS

The Milagro Beanfield War (Ballantine, 1974)
The Magic Journey (Ballantine, 1978)
A Ghost in the Music (Holt, Rinehart & Winston, 1979)
If Mountains Die (Knopf, 1981)
The Last Beautiful Days of Autumn
(Holt, Rinehart & Winston, 1982)
The Nirvana Blues (Ballantine, 1983)
On the Mesa (Peregrine Smith, 1986)
American Blood (Henry Holt, 1987)
A Fragile Beauty (Peregrine Smith, 1988)

• Matters of Life and Death •

An Interview with Raymond Carver

William L. Stull

These days, Raymond Carver and his companion Tess Gallagher shuttle between two houses in Port Angeles, a mill town and low-key resort atop Washington's Olympic Peninsula. Carver's house is a handsomely restored Victorian in a working-class neighborhood west of town, not far from the truck route, harbor, and log dump. There, in November of 1986, we discussed his fiction, with Carver stoking the wood stove against the autumn damp. The next afternoon we shifted to Gallagher's residence, an elegant contemporary in a development to the east of Port Angeles. With his back to the deepening blue of the Strait of Juan de Fuca, Carver talked about this recent poetry, much of which had been written in the glass-walled study downstairs.

Raymond Carver is the author of five collections of short stories, two chapbooks, and three volumes of poetry. He and Gallagher have collaborated on a screenplay, Dostoyevsky, and in 1986 Carver served as guest editor of the annual *Best American Short Stories*. In 1983 the American Academy and Institute of Arts and Letters selected Carver for one of its first Mildred and Harold Strauss Livings. His more recent honors include a Pulitzer Prize nomination for *Cathedral* and the 1985 Levinson Prize from *Poetry* magazine. Carver is now editing a book on Byron for Ecco Press's Essential Poets series. He spent the winter of 1987 in Syracuse, New York, working on a third book of poems and more short stories. (Raymond Carver died on August 2nd, 1988, as this book was going to press.)

The Bloomsbury Review: It's been four years since you received your Strauss Living. Has the fellowship agreed with you?

Raymond Carver: The award changed my life dramatically and irrevocably. It's let me see myself as a full-time writer. Of course, they gave me the award on the basis of my fiction, and the first thing I did was write two books of poems. But I am writing fiction again. I came out here in January of 1984 with the intention of writing fiction. After *Cathedral* was published in October 1983 there was a real hubbub going on in Syracuse, and this hubbub extended right on into the new year. It wasn't entirely unpleasant, but I was thrown off my stride, and I couldn't find my way back to my work. And I had emptied out my cupboards. I had no new work in hand after *Fires* and *Cathedral* appeared. I didn't have anything new that I was working on, and everything seemed to conspire against my writing new work. The phone was always ringing. I was trying to work, but I simply couldn't see my way clear to do it in Syracuse. For a while I thought I would try to find an apartment to work in. But then Tess suggested I come out here and work. This house was sitting empty. So I came out here with the intention of writing fiction. But when I got here I just sat and was very quiet and still for a week. I did some reading. Then on about the sixth day I wrote a poem. I can't really tell you why. I think I picked up a magazine and read some poems and thought I could do better. I don't know if that's the best motive for writing a poem, but I think it is what prompted me to begin to write poems. The next day I wrote another poem, and the next day I wrote a couple more. In two weeks I had twenty poems or so, and I just kept writing. No one could have been more surprised than I was, because I hadn't written any poetry in over two years. I would write myself out every day, and then at night there was nothing left. The bowl was empty. I went to bed at night not knowing if there would be anything there the next morning, but there always was. So somewhere in there, after I had fifty or sixty poems written and was still going, I thought, jeepers, maybe I'm going to write a book of poems. Lo and behold, I wrote poems for sixty-five days, including a poem on the day I left here. I wrote a poem in the morning and left on an early afternoon flight to go back to Syracuse. And I had my book, *Where Water Comes Together with Other Water*. In September of 1984 I started writing poems again. And I kept writing poems until February or March, and for all intents and purposes I had the poems that went into *Ultramarine*. I went back to writing stories last winter, and now all those poems seem like a great gift. I can't really account for how they happened.

TBR: Elsewhere you've said that a poet needs something more than talent in order to stand out from the crowd of MFA program graduates. What is that something?

RC: It's something to be got at beyond the poetry. I'm not sure just what it is, but it's something unmistakable in the work and it always declares itself when it's there. Rilke is quoted as saying, "Poetry is experience." That's partly it. In any event, one always recognizes the real article from the trumped-up ersatz product which is so often top-heavy with technique and intellection and struggling to "say" something. I'm tired of reading poems that are just well-made poems.

TBR: Who are some contemporary poets who achieve what you're talking about?

RC: I admire the work of Philip Levine. I like Robert Hass's poetry. He's writing about things that matter in a very beautiful, straightforward manner. Galway Kinnell is another. Hayden Carruth, Philip Booth, William Heyen, Mary Oliver, Don Justice, Louis Simpson, Tess, to name just a few. There are lots of others.

TBR: In a good many instances, you've approached what seems to be a single incident from two angles, treating it in both poetry and prose. Are there limits on a writer's experience?

RC: I don't feel I'm short on things to write about. But some things, I'm thinking of "Distress Sale" now, that poem, or the story "Why Don't You Dance?" — the yard sale situation — the idea, the image of the yard sale made such a strong impression on me that I dealt with it first in a poem and then in a story. The same thing is true with regard to the poem "Late Night with Fog and Horses" and the story "Blackbird Pie." In each instance I wrote the poem first and then wrote the story, I suppose, because I apparently felt a need to elaborate on the same theme.

TBR: Is narrative, the storytelling element, what links the genres for you?

RC: Yes. And just as I'm more interested in representational art as opposed to abstract art, I'm more interested in poems with a narrative or story line to them than in free-associating poems that don't have any grounding in the real world.

TBR: Dennis Schmitz was one of your teachers in the late sixties. Recently he commented that your poetry gets at the figurative possibilities of everyday living — seeing a snail on the garden wall or locking yourself out of the house.

RC: I'm interested in that kind of poetry, and I'm pleased with Schmitz's remark. He was for many years — and still is — an inspiration to me, even though our poetry is very different.

TBR: Your new poetry openly celebrates intimacy, and in some poems the walls between life and art seem very thin. Is there a risk of sentimentality or embarrassment in that?

RC: Any right-thinking reader or writer abjures sentimentality. But there's a difference between sentiment and sentimentality. I'm all for sentiment. I'm interested in the personal, intimate relationships in life, so why not deal with these relationships in literature? What about intimate experiences like those recounted in "A Haircut" or "The Gift"? Why can't such experiences be turned into poetry? These little experiences are important underpinnings in our daily lives, and I don't see any problem in turning them into poems. They are, after all, something that we all share — as readers, writers, and human beings.

TBR: You're not inclined to treat mundane matters ironically, then?

RC: No. I can't imagine treating them ironically or denigrating them in any way. I don't think there should be any barriers, artificial or otherwise, between life as it's lived and life as it's written about. It's only natural to write about these things. The things that count are often intimate things. I'm embarrassed for the people who are embarrassed by the idea of someone writing about things such as haircuts and slippers and ashtrays and hominy and so on.

TBR: Still, for a long time, and even to an extent today, the facts of everyday living, things like getting haircuts and picking up the mail, were thought by some to be subjects beneath the poet's dignity.

RC: But see where that's gotten us. So much of our poetry has become like something you see in a museum. You walk around and politely look at it and then go away and discuss it. It's been given over to teachers and students. And it also seems to me that of all the art forms, poetry is probably the one with the worst press, if you know what I mean. It's got the largest number of hanging judges involved on the peripheries. So many people who don't even read poetry often make pronouncements about it. These people feel that standards have been thrown out the window, the barbarians are at the gate, and nothing is sacred any longer. I don't have sympathy for guardians, so-called, of sacred flames.

TBR: You don't hold with the modernist notion that poetry needs to be difficult?

RC: Of course not. I'm saying just the opposite. My friend Richard Ford recently passed along a remark he'd heard from Joyce Carol Oates. She told him, "Ray's poems are arousing resentment in some quarters because he's writing poetry that people can understand." I take that as a compliment. I don't have a whole lot of patience with obscurity or rhetoric, in life or in literature.

TBR: Three years ago, when you reviewed Sherwood Anderson's *Selected Letters* for the *New York Times,* you quoted Anderson as saying, "Fame is no good, my dear, take it from me." What do you make of all the attention you've received?

RC: It's not unpleasant. I haven't gotten blasé about it. I don't think I'm a different person. The good things that have happened are a spur that makes me want to do more. I don't want to rest on my laurels, as it were, comfortably or uncomfortably. I feel everything is yet to be done. Speaking of his work a year ago or so before he died, John Gardner said, "When you look back there's lots of bales in the field, but ahead it's all still to mow." I feel that way.

TBR: In your essay "Fires" you acknowledge John Gardner and Gordon Lish as influences on your writing. Gardner was your teacher at Chico State, and in your foreword to his posthumous book On *Becoming a Novelist* you write about what he taught you. Lish was your editor at *Esquire* and later, for a time, at Knopf. What did you learn from him?

RC: In much the same way as John Gardner, he gave me some good advice and counsel on particular stories. He was a stickler for the right word. In that sense, I had two of the best teachers a writer could possibly have. He had a wonderful eye, an eye as good as John Gardner's, even though he and Gardner were completely different in other ways. Gardner said don't use twenty-five words to say what you can say in fifteen. This was the way Gordon felt, except Gordon believed that if you could say it in five words instead of fifteen, use five words. One of the things that was so helpful about Gordon was that he believed in me as a writer when I needed that, when I had no other contact with the great world, living as I was in Sunnyvale and Cupertino, California. He championed my work. He was constantly reading it aloud at conferences and even reprinting it when he had the opportunity. I owe him a real debt of gratitude.

TBR: Gardner and Lish may have taught you not to waste words, but you carried verbal economy to new extremes in revising the stories for *What We Talk About* from their magazine versions. You've said that you cut your work to the marrow, not just to the bone. Later, when you published alternate versions of the stories in *Fires,* you restored many of the excisions. What led you to perform such radical surgery in the first place?

RC: It had to do with the theory of omission. If you can take anything out, take it out, as doing so will make the work stronger. Pare, pare, and pare some more. Maybe it also had something to do with whatever I was reading during that period. But maybe not. It got to where I wanted to pare everything down and maybe pare too much. Then I guess I must have reacted against that. I didn't write anything for about six months. Then I wrote "Cathedral" and all the other stories in that book in a fairly concentrated period of time. I've said that if I had gone any further in the direction I was going, the direction of the earlier stories, I would have been writing stories that I wouldn't have wanted to read myself.

TBR: The Strauss award bought you time to write, but many of your recent poems suggest that time seems shorter than ever to you.

RC: I've become more aware of this in the last two or three years. But any changes that have come about in my life because of the grant have been for the good. My life seems more interesting, for one thing. I suppose I'm living the life now, and I'm usually not aware of this on a conscious level, but I'm living the life that as a young writer

I often dreamed about but never in my wildest imaginings thought could come true. Now that I'm in that life, it's fine, it's very agreeable. But I know there's a great responsibility, too.

TBR: To what?

RC: To my work. I feel like I have an extraordinary opportunity, and there's so much work to be done. When a few days go by and I don't write, things don't seem quite right, no matter how good it is otherwise. I don't feel responsible to the American Academy of Arts and Letters or beholden to anyone or any institution, you understand. I just feel it's imperative that a writer keep writing. That I keep writing. I can't imagine not writing. Oh, I suppose I could, if I felt I didn't have anything else I wanted to say. I could stop then, sure. But as long as I feel that I can write and bear witness, I intend to do so.

TBR: Writers have traditionally worked alone, but for almost ten years you've lived, worked, and collaborated with Tess Gallagher. How has this worked out?

RC: It's been very good for me, and I daresay I can speak for Tess as well. When we first got together back in 1978 she was writing and I wasn't writing. I was in the process of recovering my life. I had my health back, I was no longer drinking, but I wasn't writing. After my two books came out in 1976, there was no new work being written. And there was no new work for a good while after I got sober either. At that time I felt it was okay, it really was, if I never wrote again. I was just so grateful to have my wits back, you know. I'd been brain-dead for such a long time. And suddenly I had this other life, another chance at things. And in this new life it wasn't all that important if I wrote or not. But Tess was writing, and that was a good example for me. I was patient, and I simply waited to see what would come along, if anything.

TBR: Recently, neorealist fiction, yours included, has been faulted from the left. Some critics urge a return to the literary experimentalism of the late sixties and early seventies. How do you react?

RC: It's strange, because a number of right-wing, neoconservative critics say I'm painting too dark a picture of American life. I'm not putting a happy face on America. That's the stick they swing at me. As for the experimental fiction of the sixties and seventies, much of that work I have a hard time with. I think that literary experiment failed. In trying out different ways of expressing themselves, the experimental writers failed to communicate in the most fundamental and essential way. They got farther and farther away from their audience. But maybe this is what they wanted. Still, I think when people look back on that period fifty years from now it's going to be looked on as an odd time in the literary history of the country, an interruption, somehow.

TBR: An interruption in the course of realism?

RC: I don't really think in those terms, but now that you ask me, yes. For someone like myself, a writer in the realist tradition, it just seems that fiction about fiction or about the experience of writing fiction is not very viable or lasting. What are we doing if we're not writing about things that count, matters of life and death, as it were, to use the title of Tobias Wolff's anthology? I don't go around thinking of myself as a realist writer. I simply think of myself as a writer. But, it's true, I am trying to write about recognizable human beings who find themselves in more or less critical situations.

TBR: What makes your writing uniquely your own?

RC: Well, certainly, the tone in the work, I suppose. Geoffrey Wolff said in a review of my first book of stories that he felt he could pick out a story of mine without seeing my name attached to it. I took that as a compliment. If you can find an author's fingerprints on the work, you can tell it's his and no other's.

TBR: Where do those fingerprints lie? In subject? In style?

RC: Both. Subject and style, the two are pretty much inseparable, right? John Updike once said that when he thinks of writing a story only certain areas of writing and experience are open to him. Certain areas, and lives, are completely closed. So, the story chooses him. And I feel that's true of myself. Speaking as a poet and story writer, I think that my stories and poems have chosen me. I haven't had to go out looking for material. These things come. You're called to write them.

TBR: You're sometimes discussed as a social realist who focuses on the down side of working-class life. But, if your people are beat, they're seldom beaten. It's been suggested that your abiding subject is human endurance. Would you agree?

RC: That's a preoccupation, yes, and a writer could do worse. I'm saying he could set his sights lower. Most things that we care for pass away or pass by in such a rush that we can scarcely get a fix on them. So it's really a question of enduring and abiding.

TBR: Your work, especially the work in *What We Talk About,* is now associated with what a number of critics have termed "minimalist fiction." In 1985, *Mississippi Review* devoted a special issue to the topic, and it featured your essay "On Writing." A few years earlier, however, you tried to shake off the "minimalist" tag. What makes it stick?

RC: The more special issues of magazines that are devoted to this, the longer it's going to be around. I'll be glad to see the appellation fade so that writers can be talked about as writers and not lumped together in groups where they usually don't really belong. It's a label, and labels are unattractive to the people attached to the labels. I've stopped paying it any mind, frankly. It was an annoyance for a while, and now it's not. I admire much about many of the writers who've been labeled minimalists, and yet they're all different from each other. Each offers up his or her own pleasures.

TBR: Some critics believe that if there's one thing uniting these writers and setting them apart from other postmoderns, it's their distaste for irony. Does that ring true to you?

RC: I think they mean that these writers, the so-called "minimalists," are not ironists in the sense that there are no secrets between the sophisticated writer and the writer's sophisticated audience. And I would agree with him there. I see irony as a sort of pact or compact between the writer and the reader in that they know more than the characters do. The characters are set up and then they're set down again in some sort of subtle pratfall or awakening. I don't feel any such complicity with the reader. I'm not talking down to my characters, or holding them up for ridicule, or slyly doing an end run around them. I'm much more interested in my characters, in the people in my story, than I am in any potential reader. I'm uncomfortable with irony if it's at the expense of someone else, if it hurts the characters. I don't think that's in my stories, and I really don't see much of it in the writers who are talked about as minimalists. I strive not to do that. I think I'd be ashamed of myself if I did.

TBR: Endurance seemed about the most one could hope for in *What We Talk About When We Talk About Love.* But in *Cathedral* things began to change. In that book some of your characters seem to prosper in spirit, if not in hard cash.

RC: Yes, and as writer and a very interested bystander, I'm pleased to see this happening. A writer doesn't want to go on repeating himself, using the same characters in the same circumstances, time and again. It's not only desirable, it's healthy to move on. I'm not working any kind of conscious program in my stories, no, of course not. But it seems like every time I've finished a book there's been a clear line of demarcation. There's always been a time after I finished putting together a book manuscript when I haven't worked for a while on stories. After I finished *What We Talk About* I didn't write stories for a good long while. Six months or so. Then the first story that I wrote was "Cathedral." It happened again after *Cathedral* came out. I didn't write a story for nearly two years. It's true. I wrote poems. The first story that I wrote and published after *Cathedral* was "Boxes," which appeared in *The New Yorker.* Then five or six stories came very close together. And I feel these new stories are different from the earlier ones in kind and degree. There's something about the voice, yes. Again, speaking just as an outsider or bystander, I'm glad to see these changes at work.

TBR: What common denominators do you see in the new stories?

RC: Well, for one thing, they've all been written in the first person. It's nothing I planned on. It's just the voice I heard and began to go with.

TBR: If every story is a fresh start, is a writer's development really cumulative?

RC: I feel it's cumulative in that you know you have written other stories and poems. Work begins to accumulate. It gives you heart to go on. I couldn't be writing the stories I'm writing now if I hadn't written the ones I have written. But there's no way in the world I could go back now and write another "Gazebo" or another "Where I'm Calling From" or for that matter anything else I've written.

TBR: You wrote many of the stories in *Will You Please Be Quiet, Please?* during 1970 and 1971, when you were on your first NEA Fellowship. What did you learn about writing during that year of concentrated work?

RC: Well, to put it simply, I discovered that I could do it. I had been doing it in such a hit-or-miss fashion for so long, since the early sixties. But I discovered that if I went to my desk every day and applied myself I could seriously and steadily write stories. That was probably the biggest discovery I made. Somehow, I suppose at some deeper level, I was tapping into some things that were important to me, things I'd wanted to write about and finally was able to, without a sense of grief or shame or confusion. I was able to confront some things in the work head-on. Call it subject matter. And I suppose during that time I fastened onto or discovered a way of writing about these things. Something happened during that time in the writing, to the writing. It went underground and then it came up again, and it was bathed in a new light for me. I was starting to chip away, down to the image, then the figure itself. And it happened during that period.

TBR: What's next?

RC: I have a contract for the new book of stories, and I'm in a story-writing mood. I can't wait until I can get back to my desk and stay there. I have a lot of stories I want to write. I'm wild to get settled in here and be still.

A HANDLIST OF BOOKS BY RAYMOND CARVER

Will You Please Be Quiet, Please? (McGraw-Hill, 1978)
What We Talk About When We Talk About Love (Knopf, 1981)
Fires: Essays, Poems, Stories (Capra Press, 1983)
Cathedral (Knopf, 1983)
Where Water Comes Together With Other Water
(Random House, 1985)
Ultramarine (Random House, 1986)

• On Native Ground •

An Interview with Louise Erdrich and Michael Dorris

Sharon White & Glenda Burnside

The highly acclaimed novels of Louise Erdrich and Michael Dorris — among them Erdrich's *Love Medicine* and *The Beet Queen* and Dorris's *Yellow Raft in Blue Water* — reflect both the spiritual richness of Native American ways of life and the harshness of everyday existence on the edge of material poverty and cultural displacement. Both writers are of mixed American Indian and Euroamerican ancestry, and their writings display the diversity of both worlds, extending the vital tradition and universality of contemporary Native American literature to countless readers here and abroad. Erdrich, of German and Turtle Mountain Chippewa descent, was born in Minnesota in 1952. She grew up in North Dakota and studied writing at Dartmouth College and Johns Hopkins University. Dorris, born in 1945 into the Modoc tribe, grew up in Washington State, and he went on to study theater and anthropology at Georgetown University and Yale University and to teach anthropology to college students. The two married in the late 1970s and settled in rural New Hampshire, where they are caring for their five children, teaching, and writing, each editing, criticizing, and collaborating with the other. This interview began in New Hampshire in December of 1987 and carried over into February of 1988, after Erdrich and Dorris had returned from a promotional tour of Europe.

The Bloomsbury Review: How did you set out to become writers?

Louise Erdrich: I think that we both have always written, really. We kept journals or diaries, wrote poems and that kind of thing, or at least I wrote a lot of poetry before writing fiction. I'm from a small town. I don't think either of us had fantastic educations, but in my family there was an eccentric collection of reading material around all the time — Shakespeare and *Marjorie Morningstar* and *Classic Comics*.

Michael Dorris: We had *Good Housekeeping* at mine. When I came home from college I used to read all the short stories in *Good Housekeeping* because they were all one bath's worth apiece. We didn't have a shower, so I'd get into the tub and read three short stories and be clean.

TBR: Did you have a traditional upbringing?

LE: It was a very mixed upbringing, an awareness of family on both sides. When I grew up, my mother and father worked for the Bureau of Indian Affairs, and we lived on campus in a small town. It was German and Norwegian, and quite a few people who had Indian backgrounds came down there to work at the school. It was the kind of background you take for granted until you look back and see that there was something really quite different about it.

MD: My background was slightly more schizophrenic. My father died when I was fairly young, and so I spent part of my time living with an extended family on his side and part of my time with my mother's side of the family, which is not Indian. They're from Kentucky. My parents met at a USO dance at Fort Knox during World War II. It was a jolt to go from one family to the other. They were in very different settings, but eventually you resolve such things. I mean, most mixed-blooded people have experiences of this type. We're a kind of tribe in and of itself, almost.

TBR: Did you plan early on to go to college and to study writing?

LE: No. Michael didn't either.

MD: No, I didn't. Nobody on either side of my family had ever finished high school, so that was a great aspiration, to graduate. I thought I was going to be a rodeo star, like Rayona in *Yellow Raft*. She got thrown off the horse and won a hard-luck belt buckle, and she persisted in trying to make sense of her life. I went off and took the SAT exam.

TBR: Do you regret that?

MD: No, but it was a very strange experience, because I went off to college with a totally stereotyped idea of what life would be like in the East. I went to Georgetown, because I'd gone to a high school where Jesuits taught. I studied Greek. I went off to college in the late 1960s with the idea that people in the East wore suits all the time, and so I left all my clothes, blue jeans and stuff, which would have been absolutely appropriate, at home, and I brought along one tan suit with little silver threads all through it. My roommate took one look at it in the closet and burst into hysterical laughter, and I never went out for three years.

My family was very supportive of my going to school, but they weren't certain about what was going to happen afterwards. When I was a sophomore, I got the idea that I would go on to Operation Crossroads Africa, which I think is a program still in existence, but in those days it meant basically going off to Mali and building basketball or volleyball courts. I needed a scholarship to go, but the funding ran out. My family was willing to mortgage the house so that I could go. I never did, but that's the kind of support I had. Louise's family is the same way. Louise went to Dartmouth after her mother read about their winter carnival in *National Geographic*.

LE: Yes, my mother and father were very supportive. Once I had made it clear that I wanted to go, they helped me with all sorts of things.

TBR: How do you affect each other's writing?

MD: It's hard to draw distinctions, even with such things as plotting, because there's so much give and take. I think Louise was a much more professional writer, more aware of herself as a writer than I was, even though I'd written a couple of books by the time we started working together. But now the process of everything that goes out, from book reviews to magazine articles to novels, is a give and take. I think we're so familiar with each other's critiques and pet peeves that even when the other person isn't actually in the room, he or she is kind of perched on the other's shoulder. I now know, for example, that I often have a tendency to overstate and overexplain, and Louise keeps me honest with that and reminds me that what I'm trying to get at is perfectly clear without beating people over the head with it.

TBR: Louise, has Michael's training in anthropology brought you a greater understanding of your characters?

LE: Yes, certainly. The kinship network, for instance, is very complex. It's sort of ludicrous when we start dissecting it. Michael is trained to think about it in a very organized way, and that's been useful to both of us. We have this kinship chart for our characters in our minds, but if we wanted to, we could write it down, and Michael would know how to structure it. There is an organized mind behind the chaos.

MD: Doing ethnography in a small community is very much like puzzling out characters, which we do before we start writing.

You're confronted initially with what looks like chaos, and gradually you get to know things and realize with time that you haven't understood what the basis of relationships really was. I did my fieldwork in an Alaskan village, and I was there nineteen months altogether and was constantly trying to figure out who was who and what was going on. I don't know if I ever succeeded, but that was the process.

TBR: What has Louise's mastery of fiction taught you about anthropology?

LE: That's an interesting question. I wonder if that would help you in any way, Michael.

MD: It is an interesting question. Whereas fiction and anthropology are contributory, I'm not sure that it works in the opposite way, because in fiction you ultimately have control over the characters and the situation, and what you're bound by most of all is the consistency at the core of your characters, throughout their lives, in various situations. In fieldwork, intuition is very important, but when you are writing about people who are disenfranchised, you can't afford to speculate. You can only write about what is absolutely, unequivocally true and agreed upon on all sides. That's a responsible way to do anthropology, but I don't think it's the best way to do fiction. So I think that the work Louise does and what I try to do, in terms of figuring out characters and speaking in different voices and putting ourselves into the heads of imaginary people, would have to be left behind if I should do more ethnography. It's just too dangerous when you're dealing with real people. There are too many cases in the history of anthropology where scholars have said, "These are my people and only I really understand them, and only I can interpret them to the rest of the world," and they've been dead wrong. Many people have suffered from the presumptuousness of someone doing just that.

TBR: How much can non-Indian social workers, spiritual leaders, and so forth do to help Indian causes, especially when they cannot make that leap of understanding?

MD: The most important thing in a reservation situation is for the government to honor its treaties. There are over two hundred existing treaties between federally recognized Indian tribes and the United States, and every one of them has been kept by those tribes, while not one of them has been kept to the letter by the government. If those agreements were honored, it would create a much stronger economic and political base for the tribes and would provide a great deal more autonomy and sovereignty — and the right not only to control one's destiny, but also to make mistakes and learn from them.

One of the problems with American policy historically has been its treating all tribes as if they were the same, with uniform policies that deal with Indians as Indians, rather than as Chippewas, as Hopis, each tribe in terms of its particular history and treaty. Following the law would be the first thing that people could do. The second is to allow a long period for reacclimation, so that the tribes might achieve self-sufficiency. Beyond that, there is a need to be candid and unromantic in criticizing things that are wrong. A willingness to take positions which might be construed as embarrassing to others is occasionally necessary, whether one is Indian or white.

TBR: Who would you say is the more critical of the two of you?

MD: I guess we both are.

LE: I think we're both pretty merciless.

TBR: In your own work, you don't end up kicking each other in the shins when the other one comes along and says, "This is terrible! This doesn't work."

LE: I think it's harder to be the one who has to say those critical things. You know how hard it is to hear something critical.

MD: You don't want to bump into someone who's on a run, doing something they've finally been able to start, just because one word or sentence seems out of whack.

LE: Michael's very tactful.

TBR: Who — or what — influences your work?

MD: Well, Louise, primarily. I mean, I would not be writing if I were not working with her. Your previous work influences what you're doing. I read Barbara Pym for instruction, and for lots of different things. I don't think for me there's one particular source, except for the fact that I apprenticed with Louise.

TBR: Are the stories you write and the people you write about the ones you grew up with?

LE: No, we invent them out of our own heads. Every so often, though, there's something that comes from something that happened, or is suggested by something that happened.

MD: There are some writers who really do autobiography in the form of novels. We're not like that.

LE: It's not that we haven't tried. It was just so hard, and it turns into something else. That's one reason to admire, say, Philip Roth's novels. They seem to be autobiographical, but if you read what he writes as autobiography, you realize that these are so different and so constructed and invented that it's really a special art to make novels that play with real life.

TBR: So you didn't grow up, say, with people like the characters in *Love Medicine.*

LE: Not so that you'd recognize anyone. You know, you have to grow up with people who may say the kind of things those characters would say, or with some of those settings — especially the landscapes, which are as accurate as we could make them.

MD: Certainly we grew up in the contexts that we write about, but there is not someone particular who matches this character, someone who matches that character.

TBR: Are you breaking secrets?

MD: Well, we're making up the secrets. We would be violating only our own imaginations. None of our novels is based on real people. They are made of pure, dreamed-up characters and situations.

LE: But one of the oddest and most wonderful things that happens is that someone from a reservation we've never set foot in says, "How did you know that this was the way with my family?" or something like that. It may not be a particular incident, but the way in which the family interacts that reminds them.

MD: I think the greatest secret of all that we reveal about Indians is that Indians have a sense of humor. The one thing that Indian people have said about our books, and the greatest relief to us, is that they find them very funny. Many literary reviewers read *Love Medicine* and saw it as a book about plight and despair and poverty and tragedy, all of which is there, too. Many Indian readers saw the survival humor and the kind, odd, self-deprecating humor that Indians have.

LE: Indians have had mainly good responses to our books. Michael says that if people have bad responses, they've been kind enough not to say so.

TBR: How about the critics?

LE: We've been tremendously fortunate. There will always be some bad reviews that stick in your mind forever, but the response has far surpassed anything we could have hoped for.

MD: It's been a pleasant surprise, too, because you write a book in the privacy of your home and your thoughts and your shared feelings, and it all seems so very particular. It's such a surprise, because all of those books now have or soon will have lots of foreign editions, and the thought of people overseas reading them and finding things with which to identify in them is amazing and quite wonderful.

TBR: Do you think of yourselves as Native American writers, or as writers who happen to be Native American who happen to be writing about Native Americans?

LE: I don't know if we've made a decision about that. At least I haven't. Being Indian is something we're terribly proud of. On the other hand, I suppose that in a general sense I would rather that Native American writing be seen as American writing, that all of the best writing of any ethnic group here be included in American writing. These are university-inspired divisions so that people can have courses and concentrate on certain areas.

MD: James Welch should not be taught only in Native American literature courses. He should be taught in contemporary American and world literature courses. To pigeonhole him is to deny access to him. To lump all Indians into one literary category just because their ancestors were here before the Europeans is hard to justify.

TBR: What are you working on right now?

MD: Well, the next book out is Louise's *Tracks,* which will be out in the fall of 1988. It takes place before the action of *The Beet Queen* and *Love Medicine* and involves some of the same characters. My next book is *The Broken Cord,* about fetal alcohol syndrome, a major problem in the Soviet Union, Scandinavia, Japan, Canada, and the United States. It should be out about a year from now. And we have other more tenuous projects in the works. We have some short stories and an essay in *The New York Times Book Review* and other odds and ends.

TBR: Do you find it harder to write essays and reviews than fiction and poetry?

LE: I certainly do.

MD: I think it's easier to write fiction because I really enjoy it so. It's still very new to me. And you don't have to footnote.

TBR: One of your books is being filmed, isn't it?

MD: *Yellow Raft in Blue Water* is optioned for the movies. It has not yet gone into production. The screenwriters wrote *American Graffiti* for George Lucas, as well as a number of other films, and Sidney Pollack optioned it for his production company. There's a long distance between optioning, and writing the script, and actual production. They have to find the cast and convince themselves that there's an audience for this kind of stuff.

TBR: And that it will make money.

MD: They've "costed it" — there's a whole new vocabulary one has to learn — and it would be a moderately priced film to make. It's just that they're not sure that people want to see movies about Indians in the United States.

TBR: Is living in New Hampshire an obstacle to writing about your home in the West?

LE: No. I mean, in some ways you're fueled by nostalgia to set your story in, say, part of Montana. I can remember thinking, "Where did you come up with 'the pearl sky'?" When you go out there and look, it would be that way. I think that with memories you try so hard to recreate the landscape that things happen that are probably more interesting than what you'd expect. But I miss it. And when I was out West, I missed the woods here.

TBR: Is *Tracks* constructed in the same way as the other novels?

LE: It's more like *Yellow Raft* because it has two narrators who tell the same stories in different ways.

MD: But they're alternating, not sequential.

LE: They do alternate, rather than follow three sequential divisions. They speak in the first person.

MD: The narrators are a young girl and an old man. *Tracks* is after *Love Medicine* and *The Beet Queen,* so there's a set. Louise's next novel is tentatively entitled *American Horse.* The novel I've started, *Cloud Chamber,* is not in the first person at the moment, though it may go back. First-person stuff reads so much better in public than third-person. It's so much more dramatic and involving, and since we read these books out loud to each other so much, I think maybe that will have something to do with changing it.

TBR: With a houseful of children, how do you portion out your day so that you have time to write?

LE: We have a woman who babysits, and our older children are in school.

MD: It's fairly simple, really, except that there are so many days on which the ideal does not materialize. There are dental appointments and school vacations, this and that. One thing that keeps us going is that we always feel so lucky to be able to have a day of quiet just to sit and write.

TBR: What do you do when you're not writing or working?

LE: You know, we have children, and that seems to take care of the rest. We read, and we have hobbies that we never get around to, that sort of thing.

MD: The days are very short. We always feel that we haven't done enough at the end of the day.

TBR: What aspects of your work would you especially like your readers to understand?

MD: Well, there's a political aspect to it that I think is kind of interesting and subtle. We got a wonderful note in a Christmas card from Vine Deloria in which he said that one of the functions of people like us is to remind each successive generation that Indians exist. And he said that it's unfortunate that we, as Indians, rarely get past that thing of just reminding people that we exist. You know, some day we're going to have to deal with this. We certainly don't write polemics; we write about communities of people who happen to be Indians, but in the current political climate — in the past two presidential terms, the amount of money for Indian health care, for Indian welfare and legal assistance has declined dramatically. The number of Indians in college and graduate school has declined because the funding has evaporated. The problems of the one and a half million Indians in this country have become abstract to the population at large. If people read what we have written and identify with the characters as people like themselves, people with needs and desires and wants, that's political. That's something that we're very grateful to be able to do.

A HANDLIST OF BOOKS BY LOUISE ERDRICH AND MICHAEL DORRIS

Louise Erdrich:

Jacklight (Holt, 1983)

Love Medicine (Holt, 1984)

The Beet Queen (Holt, 1986)

Tracks (Holt, 1988)

Michael Dorris:

Native Americans: Five Hundred Years After (Crowell, 1977)

Yellow Raft in Blue Water (Holt, 1987)

The Broken Cord (Harper & Row, 1989)

About the Contributors

Tom Auer (William S. Burroughs) is the founding editor of *The Bloomsbury Review* and is now its publisher and editor-in-chief. A power forward in basketball, he makes his home in Denver, Colorado. He is writing a biography of the American publisher Alan Swallow.

Glenda Burnside (Michael Dorris and Louise Erdrich) is an editorial assistant at *The Bloomsbury Review.* She lives in Denver.

Linda W. Ferguson (Kay Boyle) is author of the nonfiction study *Canada,* published in 1981. She lives in Ramah, Colorado.

Ray Gonzalez (Robert Creeley, John Nichols, Alastair Reid), poetry editor of *The Bloomsbury Review,* is a poet and publisher who lives in Denver. He has published several books of poetry, among them *From the Restless Roots* (Arte Público Press, 1986) and *Twilights and Chants* (James Andrews and Co., 1987). He is the editor of the anthologies *City Kite on a Wire: Thirty-Eight Denver Poets* (Mesilla Press, 1986) and *Crossing the River: Poets of the Western United States* (The Permanent Press, 1988).

James R. Hepworth (Wendell Berry) is a writer and publisher who teaches at Lewis-Clark State College in Lewiston, Idaho. His work as a publisher has been honored with three Western States Book Awards, and his essays have appeared in such publications as *The Bloomsbury Review, Western American Literature,* and *The Paris Review.* He is now writing a study of Wallace Stegner's work.

Derrick Jensen (Joseph Campbell) keeps bees and coaches high jumping near Coeur d'Alene, Idaho. He writes fiction and nonfiction for both the page and oral interpretation, and he has performed his work throughout the United States.

Christopher Larsen (Douglas Adams) is a technical editor who makes his home in Media, Pennsylvania. He worked as an editorial assistant at *The Bloomsbury Review* from 1982 to 1983.

Carol Caine London (Margaret Drabble) lives on Staten Island, New York. Her work has been published in a number of journals, among them *Summerscope* and *Moviegoer*. She contributed an essay on pioneer women to Barbara Grizzuti Harrison's *Unsexing the Lie* (William Morrow, 1974).

Gregory McNamee (Wendell Berry, Bernard Mac Laverty) is a writer and editor who makes his home in Tucson, Arizona. He is a contributing editor to *The Bloomsbury Review,* and his essays, short stories, and reviews have appeared in several books and journals. He is coeditor, with James R. Hepworth, of *Resist Much, Obey Little* (Dream Garden Press, 1985) and translator, from the Greek, of Sophokles's *Philoktetes* (Copper Canyon Press, 1987).

Joe Nigg (Joseph Campbell) is the author of *The Book of Gryphons* (Apple-wood Books, 1982), *The Strength of Lions and the Flight of Eagles* (Green Tiger Press, 1982), *A Guide to the Imaginary Birds of the World* (Apple-wood Books, 1984), and *Winegold* (Wayland Press, 1985). His articles and stories have appeared in a number of children's magazines and literary journals. He lives in Denver, where he makes his living as a writer and editor.

Rodger Rapp (Barry Moser) is a contributing editor to *The Bloomsbury Review.* He has been an art reviewer for *Woodstock Times* (Woodstock, New York) and managing editor of *Satellite World,* an international telecommunications periodical. He lives and writes in Boise, Idaho, where he spends his weekends in the field as a volunteer paleontologist for the United States Bureau of Land Management.

Robert W. Smith (Farley Mowat) lives and works in Bethesda, Maryland. He has written ten books on physical education, as well as essays and reviews for *The Washington Post, USA Today, The Chicago Sun-Times,* and the *Cleveland Plain Dealer.*

William L. Stull (Raymond Carver) is associate professor of rhetoric at the University of Hartford. His essays have appeared in *Philological Quarterly, American Book Collector,* and *The Dictionary of American Literary Biography.* He is editor of T*hose Days: Early Writings* by Raymond Carver (Raven Press, 1987) and author of a forthcoming book-length study of Carver's work.

John Sullivan (John Nichols) writes and edits journalism at the *New York Daily News.* An expatriate Coloradoan, he is also a playwright.

Sharon White (Michael Dorris and Louise Erdrich) teaches English and creative writing in rural Massachusetts.

Acknowledgments

I am deeply indebted to a great many people for their help in gathering this book, foremost among them the interviewers, the writers with whom they shared these conversations, and the photographers and artists whose work is included here. All of them have been most generous in allowing me to make a book of their work. Kevin Dahl and the staff of the Tucson Public Library Infoline provided help at several points. Tom Miller, Scott Mahler, Tom Sheridan, and Ken Nichols flagged me on. To Tom Auer and Marilyn Auer of *The Bloomsbury Review* I owe countless thanks for their encouragement, many acts of kindness, and patience in attending to endless calls for help on impossibly tight deadlines. To Melissa McCormick, I am grateful for similar courtesies on even stranger deadlines, and for constant friendship.

Gregory McNamee